LESSONS LEARNED DURING THIRTY-FOUR YEARS IN LAW ENFORCEMENT

IS IT ROUTINE?

*This simple question is one that all
Law Enforcement Officers should consider and
live by as situations can and do end up
much different than anticipated.*

*This could be a life saving question
whether working as a:*

Military Policeman,

City Policeman, or

State Game Warden

Thirty-four years of law enforcement experience
with three distinctly different agencies by:

JOHN S. ORTMANN

⊘iUniverse®

IS IT ROUTINE?
Lessons Learned During Thirty-Four Years in Law Enforcement

iUniverse books may be ordered through booksellers or by contacting:

iUniverse
1663 Liberty Drive
Bloomington, IN 47403
www.iuniverse.com
1-800-Authors (1-800-288-4677)

Because of the dynamic nature of the Internet, any web addresses or links contained in this book may have changed since publication and may no longer be valid. The views expressed in this work are solely those of the author and do not necessarily reflect the views of the publisher, and the publisher hereby disclaims any responsibility for them.

Any people depicted in stock imagery provided by Thinkstock are models, and such images are being used for illustrative purposes only.
Certain stock imagery © Thinkstock.

ISBN: 978-1-5320-1883-1 (sc)
ISBN: 978-1-5320-1882-4 (e)

Library of Congress Control Number: 2017903719

Print information available on the last page.

iUniverse rev. date: 03/17/2017

"This simple question is one that all law enforcement officers should consider and live by because situations rarely end up as may be anticipated at the beginning." Following is my story about how I came to believe in this simple question through real experiences over my thirty-four year career.

Dedication

Since I began writing this book over three years ago there have been many changes in our nation, much of which has centered with our law enforcement activities in many of our communities. Here I will reflect on my past life in law enforcement and my experiences that led me to realize that what I had to endure was pretty dangerous.

That was then, but now I see what officers in all branches of law enforcement have to deal with including; social unrest, an increase in drug and narcotic use some of which may now be legal in some states, terrorism and other heinous crimes that cause the senseless deaths of many of our nation's citizens including our men and women in uniform. What we hear now is "blue lives matter" because people of all races, cultures and religions should understand and envision what our communities would be like without law enforcement. I think most of our citizens do.

The men and women who dedicate their lives and the lives of their families to protect us day and night in all manner of situations and emergencies need to be in our prayers daily. I therefore dedicate this book to all of you. Love one another, be safe, watch your partners back, and keep up your good work! May God bless you.

ACKNOWLEDGEMENT

My wife Joan deserves much of the credit for assisting me with this book. She has been my "best friend" and has supported me during all my police, game warden and retirement years as we celebrate our fiftieth anniversary this year, 2017.

And of course I thank my children of whom I am very proud. Kim, Debbie and Steve lived through my career of mid-week days off and work schedules that included almost all weekends at work and away from home. As with all children of game wardens, they learned about wildlife by helping me care for the many animals I frequently brought home for temporary care and feeding.

I cannot leave out the many people who were involved with my Christian upbringing including my wonderful parents, my wife and several pastors who have also become an important part of my life.

CONTENTS

PREFACE

This is my book and it is my story. All contained herein is true and follows my life from age twenty to my retirement age of fifty-five and now well beyond to my present age of seventy-four.

My first ride in a police vehicle was during my early teens when friends and I were transported by "paddy wagon" on Saturday mornings to little league baseball games that were supported by our city police department baseball program. I don't know if this prompted my interest in police work, but in this story I will tell about my employment with three different law enforcement agencies from the early sixties to the late nineties which collectively spanned thirty-four years.

My first formal training was as a private attending basic training, then Provost Marshall General School, or more simply military police school. After my military service and receiving an Honorable Discharge I was hired by a city police department where I received police academy training as a police officer. I later assisted by teaching future officers in a similar academy many years later while employed by a state wildlife agency as a game warden. I can say without hesitation that the combination of all the training I received while employed by these three agencies solidly formed who I am today. I'd like to tell you about my years of continuous formal and informal education and training and the experiences that led me early on to consider and believe in the importance of the title of this book, Is It Routine?

So come with me through the rest of my story as I describe more of my life, training and the various investigations, cases and people I met as I continued with my career. Their names are not mentioned as I'm sure some would like it that way and individual names are not nearly as important as the story their actions tell related to the focus of this book. They are all true accounts as I have retained most of my paperwork, manuals, photographs and arrest reports.

I also include an overview of the evolutionary changes in laws, social conditions, equipment and tactics from the early sixties to my retirement and on to the present. I know some of you younger officers will find some of these changes to be amazing and will stir up memories with others who experienced a law enforcement career during this period of law enforcement change in our great Nation.

FOREWORD

I have known the author for twenty years, all subsequent to his extensive career in law enforcement. While I knew of his prior roles I was unaware of the fascinating events that he personally witnessed and his crucial and instrumental involvement.

The author is generally a quiet, reflective type who normally does not initiate conversation, but once engaged he contributes informative, knowledgeable and worthwhile information. From reading his initial draft I can picture him alone on a night patrol scanning the area for the non-routine with 110% concentration. Also, from reading the true events it confirms what I know of the very human side of his character where he truly finds balance between religion, kindness, nature, conservation and humanity.

The events described by the author are real life and his actions, generally without prior consultation are instinctive, automatic and effective. I highly recommend this book as a great read and a demonstration of the truly necessary skills inherent in excellent performance as an officer. In this day and age of intense public scrutiny of police actions this book is an insightful read of the dedication of law enforcement officers' where ever their assigned duties may take them.

A special note: The writer of this Forward, Stan Marks, read most of the contents of this book while it was in its pre-published stage. I offered it to him not only because of our friendship but I was aware of his extreme interest in historical and other factual books. But I remain deeply saddened by his death to cancer just a few months prior to publishing "my story". I will not think about this book and this period of my life without remembering my true friend.

INTRODUCTION

I'm retired now, but during my thirty-four year career, I was employed by three separate agencies in federal, state and city governments, each with different responsibilities and focuses. While the title of this book is a very simple question containing only three words they should be words to live by for all law enforcement officers regardless of their employing agency.

The word "routine" is present in reports I received titled, "Conservation Officers Killed and Assaulted, issued by the U.S. Department of Interior, Fish and Wildlife Service, Division of Law Enforcement. Reference is made to annual reports from 1987 through 1992 where the majority of assaults occurred to officers while on "routine patrol" or when "routinely checking fishermen for their licenses". I received this report while employed by the state agency where I spent most of my career as a fish and game warden. As I grew through time and experience in the field handling many different incidents and situations I settled on one of these agencies but learned this lesson from my experiences with all three.

Even now during my nineteenth year of retirement from my law enforcement career of thirty-four years, I frequently recall situations that had unexpected, unplanned or unusual outcomes or results. I cringe when hearing about law enforcement situations from the media or officers I know today that went bad, sometimes resulting in injury or death while responding to or investigation of a "routine" situation. The news anchors sometimes begin the news segment with "what began as a routine dispatch or contact became much more as the following account shows." Many of these "routine" events that made the news broadcasts have resulted in death or serious injury to officers, suspects and/or innocent bystanders. I still hear from some of those in law enforcement today the word routine being used.

Having co-taught a class in our state police academy which also served as our department's fish and game academy, titled, "Investigative Skills and Case Development", I recall that one of the major points of this class that we prepared was to stress that an investigation begins as you prepare yourself mentally while en-route and prior to arrival at the scene. Or in other words "being focused" as you arrive. In addition, I liked to use this quote from Jim Rohn, whom I don't know but entirely agree with; "Where ever you are, be there". Don't focus on past experiences or what may happen in the future. You should not have pre-conceived ideas or a "routine" or "just checking licenses attitude" and by all means do not have "tunnel vision".

Webster defines the noun; _routine_ "as a regular, more or less unvarying procedure, customary, prescribed or habitual as in business or daily life". Is this a mindset that a law enforcement officer needs for a safe response to a possible crime scene? You and I know that the answer is "no".

It was during my early experiences in law enforcement when I realized the significance of that one word. As a result I made a simple and small printed message on a red half inch tape that I stuck on the dashboard of my patrol vehicle(s) that read; IS IT ROUTINE. It was there in front of me every time I was in my patrol vehicle as a constant reminder for me.

So now continue on and see for yourself why this word "routine" has been so important to me and why I stress to others in law enforcement to learn and make it a habit to understand that there is no such activity, situation or response that should be considered as just "routine". I hope you enjoy reading about the things I learned from some of the cases I worked and situations I was involved with during those years.

CHAPTER 1

SUMMARY OF MY TRAINING

ARMY TRAINING

Before I describe to you some of the "routine" and specific situations, investigations, and actual cases and dispositions I encountered I feel I should outline some of the training that that I received starting with basic training and military police school. Looking back I see the importance of the initial U.S. Army training that centered on physical conditioning and the discipline necessary to obey and follow orders to become part of a team.

We learned that what was good for one was good for all and of course the reverse. Each morning before breakfast we stood inspection outside of our barracks with our field packs on. Part of our required equipment we carried during the inspection was a razor. We found out why one morning as new recruits and at the beginning of our training cycle when one of our fellow recruits failed to shave prior to inspection. He had to remove the razor, not an electric razor, from his pack and shave the dry skin of his face. It was painful to watch but that problem did not recur. No one else wanted to "dry shave" at 5:00 a.m. in the morning. Another lesson we learned was when one of our team screwed up, all had to pay with additional push-ups or another lap prior to hitting the mess hall for breakfast.

I was young and fit, and loved the physical conditioning and especially the obstacle course. I received the trophy for high score achieved during the physical training and testing requirements. As a military policeman my army training continued but now included police specific topics. We were taught lots of judo and hand-to-hand combat as well as pistol, rifle and machine gun training with qualifications. I was awarded the high score trophy during the .45 caliber pistol qualifications and was rated an expert with the M-1 rifle.

I'll begin by listing more of the subjects taught during my military police training in 1963, most of which I found valuable during my continuing law enforcement career.

- Communism and Cold War Activities
- Crowd and Mob Behavior and Riot Control
- Use of Force, Apprehension and Search, Seizure and Interrogations
- Use of Chemical Agents During Civil Disturbances
- .45 Caliber Pistol Training
- M-1 and M-14 rifle training and with bayonet
- Baton, hand to hand combat with judo
- Traffic control and convoy reconnaissance
- Traffic violations and accident investigations
- Map and compass reading
- Driver training and night blackout operations
- Radio communication and "10-Code"

POLICE TRAINING

As a policeman I was assigned to attend the POST or the Peace Officer's Standard of Training academy courses in education and training required by the state with some additional specific training required due to the social unrest that really ramped up during the late 1960's while I was a civilian policeman. As you'll see my training continued through my police department years, right up to the year I retired.

The training I received as a policeman shown here is in addition to the standard police academy courses. Remember that I am talking about the mid sixties to early seventies. These subjects were very important in those days but are more important today. You'll see the importance of some of these subjects to me and our department that assisted us with our "mutual aid" relationship with surrounding law enforcement agencies.

- Civil disturbance and riot control – advanced and interagency
- Minority relations
- Anti-sniper and crowd control – field scenarios
- Chemical agent training – FBI instructed (we were required to "taste" our own medicine)
- Post academy firearms range training – FBI instructed
- Received POST Basic Certification – (was awarded after Academy graduation and four years of service)

FISH AND GAME TRAINING

My next period of law enforcement as a game warden covered a much longer period and this illustrates a variety of training subjects and opportunities for increasing job skills and knowledge. One major difference was that as game wardens we were trained to handle situations beyond that received by traditional police officers.

Much of these training subjects were district specific and provided me with additional knowledge that assisted me in the different locations of my assignments, such as desert training and snow safety awareness, just as important, I was updated with changes in technology, such as revolver conversion to semi-auto pistol training. In some areas I was an instructor for some of these subjects which I volunteered for realizing that as a trained instructor I would become more knowledgeable with the subject matter which greatly added to my confidence as my career progressed. Also, in keeping with the title of this book here is a list of training I received that helped me to make some important decisions that kept me from assuming a routine mode or attitude throughout my career.

In my later years as a game warden I received instructor assignments at our "resource academy" that ran concurrent with the "police academy" at the same location. Our academy was longer by many days and I can say without hesitation that on our graduation day many of our graduates were hired on the spot by more traditional police agencies. By the way, my son was one of these graduates. Our department was a little slow to hire so "first come, first served". I don't think he regrets it realizing that most of his weekends would be away from his family working just as he experienced with his father while growing up. Mid-week days off was still the rule with game wardens.

- Radiological monitoring (We carried a Geiger counter in our vehicles)
- Desert training with emphasis on desert safety and survival
- Boat safety enforcement – U.S. Coast Guard
- Defensive driver training – with required periodic updates
- Live-stock theft prevention – Bureau of Livestock Identification
- Search and rescue – included tracking
- Cover, concealment and movement – with night vision equipment – U.S.M.C
- Trapping Certificate of Competency – required of all trappers and wardens
- Hunter safety instructor training – required of all game wardens
- The occult for law enforcement
- Snowmobile riding safety and snow safety awareness – U.S.F.S
- Cross country skiing for patrol – U.S.F.S
- Mountain horsemanship
- Officer safety and street survival seminars – ongoing
- Verbal judo – the late George Thompson
- Hazardous materials detection, protection and clean-up – Emergency Service Office

- Incident command system – basic and intermediate course for pollution incidents
- Certified defensive tactics instructor
- Certified PR-24 (side handled baton) instructor
- **Wildlife restraint class – with five year updates (see below)**
- **Certified firearms instructor, range-master and armorer for annual inspections and repairs of department issued firearms. (see below)**
- Field training officer certification
- Certified as CPR and first aid instructor
- Received POST Intermediate and Advanced Certificates

Wildlife Restraint Class – with five year updates

A good example of a training subject listed above that I was selected to participate in that was not an expected law enforcement related activity would be our wildlife restraint class. This was conducted by our wildlife laboratory staff and wildlife management personnel whose job responsibilities included the biological studies of all the wildlife species and their habitats statewide. Some of the training that occurred during these classes took place in a local zoo where an actual need for restraint or tranquilization was on occasion asked for by the attendants.

Just think. Game wardens trained to be able to assist wildlife managers with handling many different species of wildlife by giving inoculations and drawing blood samples. We would have the ability to become familiar with their health issues and habitat facts and problems. We could use this information to assist us with our everyday search for wildlife violations and poachers.

Some of the programs that I volunteered to assist with were; net gunning deer from a helicopter to temporary restraint for biological studies, identifying parasites, fitting them with radio tracking collars to be used for continuing herd movement studies and with individual mortality studies. Also trapping and fitting mountain lions with radio collars for tracking them from the ground as well as from the air which was closely related to and an important factor in the ongoing deer mortality study. Finally tranquilizing elk with chemical darts fired from a helicopter for biological studies and sometimes for relocation.

Training in euthanasia techniques was also part of this program in fact I carried on patrol a kit with the most common euthanasia chemicals, an assortment of syringes and darts and a pistol for injecting chemical darts at longer ranges if needed. We also carried heavy duty catch poles, hobbles and blindfolds to assist with physically restraining and controlling animals of all sizes. We received calls from trappers requesting assistance when a non-target animal was caught in one of their traps and needed to be released. I used catch poles to restrain mountain lions to enable their release from leg hold traps where the take of lions was not authorized. Two guys worked best here!

Game wardens dealt with euthanasia issues quite often. A road hit deer, elk or bear with resultant life threatening injuries would normally be euthanized to end the animals' suffering. We used the method that would be the most appropriate and quick acting for each situation.

Keep in mind that euthanizing any animal while in the public view was most times done differently than if done in a location that would not be observed by others. Use of firearms for larger mammals and other mechanical means for smaller species could be methods of choice for important reasons.

Use of a firearm or other mechanical means allowed for the possible use of meat for consumption by needy citizens but most likely the carcass was able to be placed into an area close by where other wildlife could feed from it. If euthanized by chemical means the animal and all parts would have to be placed into a pit and covered with dirt and buried that same day so the residual effects of the chemical used would not adversely affect any animals including birds that may feed on it.

Let me end this part with an anecdote that really got my attention the first time I was harnessed to the outside of a helicopter during a

tranquilizing effort of elk for
relocation. The three occupants
of the helicopter all had jobs,
the pilot, the shooter and the
prep person for loading the
darts with the chemicals. I
noticed taped against the back
of the pilots' seat a syringe that

contained a clear liquid. I was told, and no joke, that in the event of
an accidental discharge of a dart into any of the three occupants the
"reversal" drug contained in the syringe would need to be immediately
injected into that person to negate the effects of the tranquilizing
drug. I really respected this decision, especially when considering the
vulnerability of the pilot.

**Certified firearms instructor, range master and armorer for
annual inspections and repairs of department issued firearms**

Our wildlife agency required of all game wardens, periodic
firearms training and qualifications. As a firearms instructor and
range master for our group of wardens located in a fairly isolated
geographic area of our state for the last fourteen years of my career,
I feel compelled to tell you what was required and how we met and
even surpassed those requirements during our training sessions.
Some of our training was a direct result of the after action reports of
police involved shooting situations nationwide where lessons needed
to be learned by officers who may be involved in similar situations.

Even though we sometimes used "shooting ranges" that were
available to us we conducted most of our firearms training as well
as other training in a state
owned and secure forest area
where we used our own targets
and portable frames to use for
our training and qualification
courses. We also had the ability
to create scenarios to address
specific training objectives.

When on the range we sometimes combined defensive tactics with our shooting to increase our stress and breathing prior to running to the shooting area. Training conducted during a two to three day campout allowed us to accomplish lots of our training goals as well as a great time for information exchanges and to grow our team relationship.

Here is an outline of our required qualification shoots where passing scores were necessary or remedial training initiated as necessary. Any training conducted with our duty and undercover side arms required service ammunition not re-loads or down loaded rounds made for target practice.

- Duty sidearm: one qualification course and at least one other training course per quarter plus two night qualification courses per year.
- Undercover sidearm: one qualification course per year.
- 12 gauge shotgun: two qualification courses per year.
- Rifle: one qualification course per year.

Some things we saw from other agencies that were somewhat puzzling. To cancel a scheduled qualification shoot because of inclement weather was pretty strange. What's up with that? So skipping training and going back to patrol in the same bad weather conditions was okay?

We qualified in rain, snow, wind, hot sunny weather while wearing the uniform we wore on patrol. Did we wear gloves in winter with temperatures well below freezing while out of the vehicle checking trappers, hunters or others? If so, we qualified with gloves on. The same went with heavy coats that covered the duty or gun belt. We didn't begin the course by taking off parts of the uniform that we would be wearing when talking to or confronting someone. Make sense? Some officers learned the hard way but that's how we learn.

We also worked on drawing, shooting and reloading with the weak hand as if our strong or gun hand, arm or shoulder took a round or was otherwise incapacitated. We got pretty good at it. What about firing a 12 gauge shotgun with one hand or weak hand only? Not fun but we did it. Again, we tried to be aware of actual shooting situations where lessons were learned by others the hard way.

CHAPTER 2

MILITARY POLICE - U.S. ARMY
1963-1965

BEGINNING OF MY SERVICE

My time in the military was during the "Cold War" which was essentially between the Korean Conflict and the Vietnam War. We faced dangers but not the warfare and terrorism combat that continues to this day. We were still trained to expect that stuff could happen so vigilance was instilled in all of us as we carried out our duties. The Soviet Union was flexing its' muscle in Eastern Europe during the early sixties and just prior to the beginning of the hostilities in Vietnam.

My Dad had served in the U.S. Army during WWII then worked for the U.S. State Department in Persia (Iran) during the time I was born. My older brother served overseas during the time of the Korean Conflict also with the U.S. Army. My wife's parents served during WWII and met on a hospital ship in the Mediterranean Sea just off the coast of Italy. I was proud to follow their lead in service to my country.

The "draft" was going strong and since I was not really into my studies at a city college and used my two years of football eligibility I decided to volunteer for the draft. I was able to get the police training I wanted and also got my station of choice, which was Europe.

Some of the men that I trained with received their first assignment to Vietnam and some of them did not return home. My heart goes out to those men and their families and also to all who served during the pre and post 9-11 hostilities and the sacrifices they and their families made and are still making and recovering from if they even made it home. Two of my good high school buddies were drafted into the U.S. Marine Corps shortly after I was discharged and they served in Vietnam. Another good friend from high school served as an Army Ranger whose service was another that our nation can be proud of. We still get together even though state lines and hundreds of miles separate us.

I can say without reservation that my initial law enforcement training as a recruit in the U.S. Army and selection to attend the Provost Marshal General School where I was trained as a military policeman was the very important first step that guided me to choose a career in law enforcement.

I served in Europe and even though I wasn't assigned to a unit to do typical police duties I was still a well trained, armed soldier involved in safety and security. We were tasked to provide security at a nuclear facility as well as provide safety and security to convoys that moved nuclear "material" from base to base and to various airfields. In 1961 the infantry conducted these duties but in 1963, the year I arrived, the western european security responsibilities were reassigned to the MP Corps. Most of the soldiers in our company were draftees and the rest of us either enlisted or like me volunteered for the "draft".

There were five platoons in our company and we were separated only by our assigned living space or quarters. Our platoon lived in a Quonset hut structure with aluminum siding and roof. It had plastic windows and a large area at one end for showering, washing and other needs. The toilet area had no partitions to separate the several stools and urinals so we got real close to our comrades.

After my first year overseas, I was promoted to corporal and became the squad leader over eight other soldiers all older and "wiser" than I.

CONVOY DRIVER

The most interesting assignment I had was as a driver for truck convoys from our facility to many other parts of Western Europe. I used an M-38 jeep to drive the convoy commander on several occasions. He and I were required to "pre-drive" or scout an upcoming convoy route in order to identify problems such as road work or other detours that may exist requiring a change in the convoy route. Also the size of our trucks prevented access through some of the small towns and villages so we would have to find a route to completely go around them.

We stayed overnight at designated military bases or air fields sometimes belonging to other countries where continuous security was provided by our own personnel. The main rule was that the convoy would never stop while traveling from one secure base to the next except for refueling from our own fuel truck. We had our own truck repair and maintenance crew as well as a communication van with us and even a truck that carried the capability to physically destroy the secret contents of the convoy if we came under attack. Constant communications were maintained with various headquarters and on some convoys there were air surveillance flights and of course we carried with us "C-rations" for meals when not at a base station.

The Soviet Liaison Group would often times be seen along our routes, taking pictures and making notes. They monitored military traffic throughout Europe. The vehicles were identified by distinctive license plates and their presence was allowed probably by some strange agreement. I considered this as exciting stuff during my young life of twenty-one and twenty-two years.

VEHICLE TRAINING

There were some learning experiences I encountered that could be called by some to be routine but growing up in the part of a state that had mild winters with no snow I quickly discovered how to drive on icy, snow covered roads and during blizzard conditions. After a few "minor" mishaps I got confident enough to expand my military driver's license from jeeps and three quarter ton trucks to heavier trucks called deuce and a half's or two and a half ton trucks. These were used to transport platoon members to their work stations during shift change at our home base and to transport fellow soldiers to other locations if needed.

SECURITY AT NIGHT

One night well after mid-night while working graveyard shift and at my assigned post I heard two gun shots from further back in the forest where others were assigned to provide security to another group of storage bunkers. We carried fully loaded M-14 rifles while on post to be able to protect ourselves and respond if necessary to unauthorized intruders. We used a designated "password" and "response" protocol that was changed prior to each shift to enable us to identify persons we encountered in the darkness or persons we did not recognize.

My first thoughts after hearing the shots were; "an intruder shooting at one of us or maybe an intruder being shot at". I remained on post but was more vigilant as our instructions clearly required. We had no means of communication so contact with each other was out of the question.

A short time later we were each contacted at our posts by our guard commander. He stated that there was no "intruder situation" and for us to carry on with our duties with a briefing to be conducted after shift later in the morning back at headquarters.

At our debriefing after being relieved by the day shift, we learned that the two shots that were fired in close proximity to the suspected intruder were enough to turn the intruder around. He then went over the fence and rapidly exited the area.

The intruder was actually a new lieutenant recently assigned to our company. He reported to the base commander that the action taken against him was "inappropriate" as soon as he returned to base headquarters. He had many scrapes, cuts and scratches but no bullet wounds. He was severely reprimanded and received his first lesson about our security and required response. Our crew received a good rating for our diligence that early morning but it took a while for our new lieutenant to feel comfortable with us. A few months later I was recruited to drive him on several convoys. We got along pretty well.

UNKNOWN EXCITEMENT TO COME

The idea of unusual and sometimes exciting stuff became part of this next "routine" assignment. Early one morning we were ordered to suit up in full combat gear, secure our weapons and ammo and prepare for immediate transportation to another facility at an unknown location.

Upon arrival about an hour and a half later we were given our assignment to set up a tight perimeter around this other nuclear facility that was similar to but smaller than ours but also located deep in the forest. We learned of the reason for our presence when we were issued badges to wear that would indicate the amount of radioactivity we would be exposed to while in this zone.

It was a long day but the problem was taken care of without injury or dangerous exposure to any of us. Apparently there was some damage observed on a warhead and it was unknown if there was something intentional going on.

LOSS OF PRESIDENT KENNEDY

A sad event that took place soon after I got to Germany was the assassination of President Kennedy, November 1963. I was working graveyard shift again in an isolated area when the news came to us that early morning our time. We were put on full alert for the entire next day and stood our posts without food, drink or much information. All we knew was the entire U.S. Military was put a high level alert until the details of the assassination could be determined and disseminated to posts overseas.

CHAPTER 3

START OF MY FAMILY LIFE -1965

The same year I was discharged from the army I met Joan on a "blind date". A week later we started dating and we haven't stopped. Talk about not "routine". Many of us have been on "blind dates" that most of the time ended after saying "goodnight". That was the "routine", right? This last "blind date" for me was a last minute date arranged by her nursing school friends and has now lasted fifty-one years and still going strong. After that first night neither I nor Joan thought it would be different than other "routine" dates. I think this may have been the beginning of my thoughts about situations "not being routine" and unanticipated.

Almost a year later she accepted my proposal. Our courtship continued, mostly weekend dating as we lived fifty miles apart and I was required to live in the city where I was employed as a police officer and she was in her last year of college. We married in 1967

after I passed my first year probationary period and her receiving her diploma as a registered nurse. I was able to convince her to go camping for our honeymoon where I found out that she liked to fish as well cook over a camp stove.

Our first residence was in the city where I was a policeman and where she became a nurse in the local hospital. Our careers during our first four years of marriage sometimes intertwined as she worked the emergency room of the hospital, a place I frequently visited during the course of my duties. She stills tells me today that she had to hide her name badge at times when I would bring in a suspect for treatment.

She supported me during some later discussions about pursuing a change of law enforcement agencies to fish and game so together we made a big step in our lives. This was a huge adjustment as we relocated hundreds of miles away to a very different climate and far removed from both of our parents as well as major changes in duties and responsibilities.

She learned early on that as a game warden I may schedule a work day or be called to work and say, "see you later" as I leave but she could never depend on a scheduled time for my return. One example; I gave her lots of worry and grief during an extended investigation that took me to a remote area where I had no outside communication, no cell phones or portable radios in those days. I was fine but because she had no way of knowing she contacted my supervisor with her concern for my welfare. Upon returning home much later that night I didn't handle it well. She didn't report me "missing" anymore. We lived through it and I love her more because of her unending concern and support for me.

By this time we had three children two girls and then we finally got my boy. They got to learn about wildlife from the animals that we are often times required to temporarily care for and feed because of seizure for illegal possession or turned in or found because of illness or injury. I recall keeping for short periods various birds the largest being a golden eagle. Also fawns and desert tortoises frequented our yard. They have more than earned my praise with how they have actually thrived and have become very caring, responsible, and loving adults.

CHAPTER 4

CITY POLICEMAN AND DETECTIVE 1966-1970

JOB REQUIREMENTS AND INITIAL TRAINING

 After my release from active duty and realizing that law enforcement was my future I was hired as a police officer in an urban city with a multi-ethnic population of about 30,000. The physical requirements for new officers at that time were male, minimum of 5'10 with weight in proportion to height and 20-20 vision with no color vision impairment. As with our community our department was also multi-ethnic and my initial training supervisor was a highly respected black sergeant.

While with this agency I received the required education and training by attending a Peace Officer Standards of Training (POST) certified police academy. Special note here: I was assigned to the academy ten months after I was on the job, meaning that I worked solo patrol for much of the ten months prior to being "officially" trained and educated as a police officer. Of course I received "on the job" training during my first few weeks after being hired; however, I was initially assigned to the graveyard shift, where I was under the delusion that "not much happened" during that midnight to 8:00 a.m. shift. "That's where we can train you for the real police work", is what I was told.

MY FIRST COUPLE OF DAYS

I'll start here with some unexpected duties assigned to me while a police "rookie". My very first day, I was sent to the major on and off ramp to the freeway that ran through our city, to direct traffic due to an accident. I was glad to have received traffic control training during my army training so I was able to handle this pretty well. The only problem I had was trying to adjust my new helmet to fit my head.

This next one is pretty funny and showed me what out of uniform work can entail and what unusual and non-routine meant. Another rookie and I were told to show up for work at 7:00 a.m. the next morning out of uniform and dressed like a laborer. We had been on the job for less than a week and wondered what kind of assignment we were in for but excited none the less.

When we showed up at the office to meet with the captain the next morning this is what we were told; "men, the city maintenance workers went on strike today and a water main that has been leaking in the middle of one of our streets is scheduled for repair. The laborers will not be here but management will be able to fix the leak once it is exposed. You will learn to use a jack-hammer to get through the asphalt then use shovels to dig up and expose the water pipe so it can be repaired. There is a city truck out back waiting to take you there."

Well, all I could relate to about jack-hammers was watching them being used in my neighborhood as a youngster, pretty cool at that time but maybe not so cool then when the very noisy and vibrating tools were in my hand and cutting through the asphalt near my feet and my used to be shiny boots.

Another example of an unexpected "call to duty" that all law enforcement officers can face while off duty is witnessing a criminal act. Some could be life threatening situations such as motor vehicle accidents, assaults, or even a rape in progress that you will read about later on, while others may be a simple assault or misdemeanor theft while shopping. I made a few arrests of shop lifters while I was off duty and doing my own shopping. It was expected of the officers of our department to be armed and prepared to handle situations or assist fellow officers while off duty.

I also found out about the misnomer "routine patrol" right away. I was "played" with during my first few months as a "rookie". I received several calls to a residence in the middle of the night to respond to the report of a "prowler". The report would be about a strange man looking in the window of a home occupied by a young woman. I was very serious about it the first couple of times but then I found out that the young woman wanted to know who the new policeman was. I did get to know her and her friends later on. Another test of my skills came when an off duty detective saw me while he was on his way home late one night. He was speeding, ran a stop sign then tried to evade me. I caught up with him in front of his home and he couldn't stop laughing. I guess I passed that test.

Much of my informal training was simply to meet with my sergeant after I conducted an investigation or handled a call so he could answer questions, give suggestions and approve my notes prior to my making the official report. After an investigation, or the completion of a request for service or answering a complaint, we went to the closest or handiest pay phone and called the station to record the report for dictation. It took a while for me to get comfortable with this procedure but each day got better and I realized that it allowed an officer to remain in his patrol area without having to go to the station removing him from the public eye when to be seen was thought of as a deterrent to illegal activity.

It was department policy that officers conduct their assigned investigations from beginning to end. We had a few specialized detectives to handle murder, serious burglary, forgery crimes and a narcotics officer who coordinated with state and federal agents for many of the drug investigations. There was no field training officer program in those days just direction from the shift sergeant or in some cases the lieutenant or captain. I was pretty active during my pre-academy months so I had to excuse myself from several academy training days because of my required testimony in court appearances.

After graduation from the police academy and three and a half years assigned to the patrol division, I was promoted to detective. There was a little more paperwork involved and I investigated some of the more difficult cases and coordinated pending cases with the district attorney's office for prosecution. This position provided me with valuable learning experience and still required me to be available night or day.

CHAPTER 5

LEGAL AND SOCIAL
CHANGES OF 1966

RIGHTS FROM MIRANDA VS ARIZONA DECISION

A short time after being hired as a city policeman was a very important time for law enforcement nation-wide because of two distinct occurrences. One was the court decision of Miranda versus Arizona and the second was the "birth" of the Black Panther Party. This year started another important first but in the sports world. The 1966 NFL season ended with the first post season playoff game between the Packers and the Chiefs on January 15, 1967. This was later named Super Bowl 1. As I write this in 2017 both the Packers and the Chiefs were in the running again but didn't quite make it.

I begin with the very important and wide reaching legal decision that was enacted by the U.S. Supreme Court in 1966. This was the case of Miranda versus Arizona. It gave protection to suspects in custody or in a custodial situation from self incrimination and provided them with the right to have an attorney present during any questioning or interrogation.

It took a few years for the true meaning and effect to law enforcement and the court system to become what was to be the way of life from that point on. It wasn't long after the decision was rendered before we were issued wallet size cards with the written rights and warnings on them that could be read to suspects without error or omission.

We were asked during court trials what "Miranda" rights were provided to the suspect as that was always one of the first issues brought before the court. It was best to read from the same card that you read to the suspect than to maybe get nervous or confused during the defense attorneys examination. I always had the laminated warning card in my shirt pocket just below my badge. I still have it but of course don't carry it with me.

BIRTH OF THE BLACK PANTHER PARTY

The Black Panther Party was also established in 1966 in a city within fifty miles from us. It was initially established for self defense especially with regard to civil rights issues and stemming from the Watt's Riots of late summer of 1965. During the active years of the "party" they initiated some community social programs that spread nationwide along with their "Black Power" movement that spawned many violent confrontations with the police of many different agencies and locations.

We were affected because of our proximity to the most active location at their start-up. Visits from "party" leaders to our city occurred but other than some demonstrations and destruction of their own businesses and property we survived.

They were permitted by our city to conduct their own "citizen patrols" in a large residential area. Our city "fathers" issued them vehicles for these patrols but this exercise in cooperation didn't last too long. A drag race and ensuing crash of two of the city pick-ups late one night ended that episode of cooperation. I was in on that investigation and it wasn't hard to determine the cause. Thankfully there were no fatalities. The majority of the citizens of that area wanted to see the return of the police officers on their streets. The further intent of the "party" by their own admission was to evaluate the behavior of all police officers when dealing with activity involving members of the black community.

CHAPTER 6

EXPERIENCES OF
MY POLICE YEARS

Several situations helped fill my experience "basket" during my police years. Although I recognize that lessons learned from actual situations continue through an entire career I have listed here just a few that still come to my mind long after my retirement.

DESCRIPTION OF OUR CITY

First, some information about the city where I spent my police officer time is included as I find it useful to tell you about it here. The downtown area and business district that included the major restaurants, bars, card rooms, and hotels was separated from the rest of the city that consisted of residential and newly modernized businesses by three railroads and their separate tracks. There were no overhead trestles or bridges close-by meaning that when the tracks were in use, which was frequently, the main roadway to downtown was temporarily closed.

When a train blocked the road for greater than fifteen minutes we took down the identifying information and gave it to our city attorney who then filed charges against the railroad. This didn't solve the problem but it provided our city with a little extra money. I don't recall the amount of the fine but the serious problem we had as officers was not being able to use the road especially during a request for emergency services on the other side of the tracks. It sometimes put the downtown beat or patrol area tough to get to in case of a situation where the officer needed assistance.

You've probably heard the term "hobo jungle", well we had one. The trains were mostly freight trains and were free rides by the homeless and other transients. Our "jungle" which was in a secluded area just out of the downtown area was home to several "hobos". Many were seasonal guests. They were not criminals but caused problems when they walked into town because of their poor personal hygiene habits and frequent drunkenness.

They were occasionally targeted by local young people hoping to find something of value on their person or in their camps. None of us wanted to have to arrest a "hobo" and place them in our patrol vehicles although sometimes we had no choice. Some of us found a way to "care" for them in a different way especially in the cold and damp winter season. In town and close to where they liked to hang out there was a television and appliance store. In an alley behind this particular store they kept their empty large cardboard shipping boxes. We would use them to tuck them in for the night and by business opening the next morning they would be gone. They used newspapers shoved in under their clothes as insulation to keep warm during cold spells.

Here is a story about our most frequent "client". He would ride the rails and end up with us for the winters. He had a history of being arrested for "drunk in public" in several locations. His record was available to us via his rap sheet. We found out this fifty plus year old man was well educated with a college degree from a highly regarded university.

One night he was unusually unruly and went to several different bars. The report of his behavior and condition necessitated his arrest and transport to our "drunk tank". The next morning when he was transferred to a cell for his donut and coffee breakfast he complained of a painful foot. Upon checking to see if medical care was needed we found he had a large open wound that he apparently had for quite a while. This was the first and only time I saw maggots in a wound of a live person.

FIRST WARRANT ARREST

My first but certainly not the last arrest of a man wanted on a felony arrest warrant took place in a black residential area adjacent to downtown. I didn't know at the time but learned from future contacts and arrests that he was a heroin addict. Each time he returned from the county jail after serving a year or so it was obvious that he spent most of his time while incarcerated lifting weights. He kept getting bigger and bigger and had a history of eluding and running from us when we attempted contact.

I saw him walking on the sidewalk and I stopped, got out of my patrol car and quickly approached him. He didn't flee but when I confronted him with my intention to serve the arrest warrant he started to consider his options. I put "hands on" which he didn't expect and the fight was on. Luckily it wasn't a boxing type fight but wrestling and I was able to subdue him, cuff him and get him into my car. At the station and after booking, printing and photographing I looked at my wrist to see what time it was. No watch. This was the beginning of a bad rest of the day for me.

I returned to the site of the arrest and there were several teenagers milling around the exact location of our "scuffle". I was glad they weren't there during the arrest. I asked if any of them had seen a wrist watch as I looked myself along both sides of the sidewalk. Of course none of them saw it. I'm sure it was long gone so didn't pursue it other than asking if someone found it would they please turn it into the police department. It never showed up. I guess I should have offered a reward.

Well, I went home to exchange my uniform shirt for one that was not dirty and torn then returned to patrol. That evening after my wife came home from her shift at the local hospital I had to tell her that her wedding present to me had been lost and or stolen earlier that day. I stressed that I wasn't hurt in an attempt to divert conversation from the lost watch. The watch was inscribed with "We Are One" and with our wedding date. From then on an inexpensive sport watch was my choice.

CANINE (K-9) RESPONSE TO BURGLARY

As some of us officers would frequently do, I accompanied a graveyard officer on his patrol after being relieved from my swing shift. We did this on weekends just for the assistance and in my case to increase my knowledge through additional experience. No extra pay was even thought about. This officer was one of our canine officers and was someone I respected and always learned from. During a response to a burglary alarm from a downtown business he let his dog loose into the dark building to search for a suspect(s). As we quietly listened and as the well trained dog searched the interior we heard a voice say, "nice dog, good boy". I don't remember the young burglar getting hurt, just some torn clothing but he was arrested without incident. He was glad to see us and said, "Just keep that dog away from me".

SHOT FIRED JUST INCHES FROM MY HEAD

I was again on an after shift patrol with the same canine officer. It was a weeknight and pretty quiet. We were slowly patrolling the downtown streets and alleys among some three to four story buildings, mostly older hotels housing permanent residents, when a loud bang broke the silence of the night.

The large red light on the light bar directly above my head at the same time shattered from a gunshot. My partner drove us out of there quickly as we didn't know where it came from but certainly didn't want to remain for a subsequent shot. We called for some help and after searching the area and buildings were unable to pin down from where the shot was fired or any other evidence concerning the shooter. The distance of the shot from my head was awful scary. My wife first learned about this among other events in my career as she helped me with editing "my story" many years after my retirement.

John S. Ortmann

HANDCUFFS NOT BIG ENOUGH!

Have you ever looked at the size of the opening of the issue handcuffs that all officers carry? They seem to be plenty big enough to go around a person's wrist, right? I thought so too but it didn't take me long to find out that there are really some big wrists out there especially on a huge man I got to know. He was employed as a "hod carrier" so was always using his hands and arms at work. He was a loner and liked to drink as soon as he got off work and for some reason was prone to get into physical altercations quite often probably because of his intimidating size.

One evening I was dispatched to a downtown bar concerning a disruptive man who was drunk and they requested that he be removed. Here came my introduction to this "gentle giant".

A side note. This call reminded me of a similar incident that occurred when I was in the army a few years prior. A small group of us got together for an excursion to Paris, France. We stayed in a downtown hotel, I'm not sure where, and one evening I took off on my own and found a bar with some local color. At twenty-two years old and with a few beers on board I became involved in a barroom scuffle with a drunk that the bartender couldn't handle. I ended up removing him from the bar to the sidewalk with some applause I might add. This American soldier made some friends and ended up with a few free beers in return

I now return to my contact of the "gentle giant". When I entered the bar I immediately saw the problem. He certainly came under the "drunk in public" statute so I tried to convince him to exit the bar with me by gentle talking. I used the tact of "hey big guy I'm just doing my job here and trying to keep you out of trouble, let's go out front and talk". He obviously had some common sense left so he accompanied me to the sidewalk in front of the bar and alongside my patrol car.

There was a lot of aggressive tension inside and they kept directing foul shouts toward him. I knew he would not leave on his own accord. I gave him the spiel of "for your own protection and before the owner decides to sign a complaint against you I'd like to take you with me to the station where you can sober up". Luckily, he was one to respect my authority and this night he was very compliant, or drunk. I conducted my search and finding no weapons or drugs put him into handcuffing position near my rear door.

I tried a couple of different times to get one of my cuffs around his left wrist but realized that they weren't going to fit, not even close. We didn't carry plastic flex cuffs in those days so I then made the decision due to his compliance to ask him if he would ride peacefully with me to the station without cuffs. I didn't wait for an answer and without further discussion I got him into the patrol car and we made the trip to the station and subsequent incarceration in the "drunk tank" without incident.

A follow-up incident with the same man a year after came when I was dispatched to a fight in one of the dark and narrow alleys downtown. Upon arrival, the fight was in progress but my "friend" the "hod carrier" was greatly outnumbered by four to one. I never knew if he had any friends. No one could take him alone that's for sure and they were using a two by four on him and both of his arms and head were bloody from the blows.

I broke it up by my presence more than anything physically I could do. He was in pretty bad shape but still standing. The crowd that had formed was still fired up so I got him into my patrol car and immediately took him to our hospital emergency room in the center of town. I knew he would get good care because my wife was the emergency room nurse on duty at that time. He and I never met officially again but I think he appreciated our relationship.

My wife later told me that when I came to the hospital with arrestees or victims for treatment, some of whom, of course didn't like me, she would put her hand over her name badge.

Because I am talking here about our local hospital I'll add another anecdote. The hospital was located at the edge of a "troubled" residential area that became part of the social unrest problems we faced in the last half of the 1960's. Gunfire was fairly common especially after dark so we would alert the hospital staff to close their blinds and shades and stay away from windows.

Another common event they dealt with was the drop off for treatment an over dose victim or others seriously injured by criminal activity. They would be deposited on the front lawn and then a phone call would be made to the hospital staff. We tried to have a presence there when we could with some officers even taking their lunch or dinner breaks there. They really appreciated it and the officers appreciated the opportunity to get out of the public eye if only for a half hour.

SUICIDE ATTEMPT DISCOVERED DURING AN INVESTIGATION

During a criminal investigation that involved a couple that lived in a county area just outside our city limits I was "nominated" to assist one of our sergeants in an attempt to locate the suspects to continue our investigation and if warranted, make arrests. He made the proper notification to the county of jurisdiction of our intent so we proceeded to a run-down mixed race neighborhood of old shacks and trailers each of us arriving in our own patrol cars.

Upon our arrival there were several people hanging around, most were unemployed except for their criminal activities. Finding the right trailer, we went to the door but got no response. One of the "on lookers" said "he's gone but she's inside". After a few more minutes attempting to get her to open the door for us, she came to the door.

She opened it but said nothing. She was white, thirty years old, fully clothed and bleeding profusely from both wrists. It was obvious she had just cut them as there was a trail of blood leading back to the bathroom. She probably had a change of heart so decided to open the door otherwise she probably knew she was a goner. We got her back inside and located enough first aid supplies in the trailer to make pressure wraps for both wrists stemming the flow of blood.

We then called for an ambulance as there was no 911 system at that time. We were advised that the ambulance would be delayed so my sergeant told me to transport her to the county hospital for emergency treatment and for a seventy two hour hold as the county hospital had a psychiatric ward. I placed her under arrest stemming from our initial investigation and transported her. Upon admittance she was placed on a seventy two hour hold because of her suicide attempt and we made arrangements for a follow-up contact with her upon her release. We would then follow-up with the investigation at that time.

Due to her medical and psychological issues that were quite serious the criminal proceedings were delayed and further disposition was handled "out of court".

MAKING FRIENDS WHILE ON PATROL

As a new officer in the community I developed what I felt was a rapport with several people of all races and backgrounds, some with interesting criminal histories. I learned that you never know who may be there to help you in a time of need and I also learned that these same people sometimes needed unofficial as well as official assistance as well. Some of the unusual places where I sought this kind of relationship were in the downtown clubs, card rooms, hotel lobbies and neighborhoods where I felt welcomed.

Prostitution and gambling was the main draw to our downtown area most all nights. Many of our visitors from out of town came "shopping" here. In one particular club known for eager "ladies of the night", I had developed a "lady" contact who was probably the "madam" in charge. I felt that she respected me for doing my job. I could go into this club on weekend nights and she would let me know of anything stirring or in the wind that could affect me or her and her friends, after all, trouble could seriously affect their business. I told my wife of her as I didn't want this contact to come to her in a wrong way. We still remember her unusual name.

Also while driving through a relatively quiet and run-down residential area I stopped many times and talked to a young black couple who frequented their front porch with their young child. Just light hearted chatter but I felt good about this contact and maybe future friendship.

One afternoon after talking with him earlier that same morning I received a dispatch to contact the post office downtown to take a report of the suspected forgery of a stolen postal money order. Upon arrival, I was told the suspect entered the post office and asked a clerk to cash a $100 money order. The clerk checked the money order against a list of those reported as stolen and found it listed as having been stolen during a burglary of a post office in a city about fifty miles away. The suspect became nervous and quickly left the post office leaving the money order on the counter.

Upon receiving his description and the description of his clothing I immediately recognized him as the man I had spoken to earlier that day.

I went to his home and he was sitting on the porch outside as he so often did and as if nothing had occurred since my last visit. We spoke briefly and I advised him of my reason for the contact. He admitted being at the post office a short time ago and went on to admit his guilt in this matter. I felt like he didn't want to lie to me because of our short but friendly relationship. I arrested him and took him to the station where he was interrogated by postal inspectors. They accompanied him to his home where he handed over a plastic bag containing twenty three additional $100 money orders and various types of identification that wasn't his. He was remanded to the custody of the U.S. Marshall's Office.

FOOT PURSUIT WITH INOPERABLE REVOLVER

One pursuit I will never forget, not because of something great I did but rather a dumb thing I did that was embarrassing for me. It was something I will describe now but certainly did not bring it up for discussion during my younger days as a police officer.

While patrolling in my favorite black and white patrol car in a predominately black residential area during the graveyard shift where known drug users, burglars and thieves resided, I observed a young male who I had encountered previously as a suspect in a rash of burglaries in the nearby business district. There was an outstanding felony warrant for his arrest for a prior burglary so I contacted dispatch to advise them of my observations and my intent to contact him.

It was winter time, cold and raining. He was wearing dark clothing including a hooded sweat-shirt and it was obvious that he tried to keep his identity hidden from me as he walked in the general direction of his home. It had been raining off and on for several days so all the exposed, unpaved ground was wet, soggy and muddy and in some places with deep puddles.

In addition, this area was without night lighting probably because all of the street lights had been shot out in order to keep unwanted eyes from seeing the activities that took place in the neighborhood after dark. As soon as I slowed my vehicle, he upped his pace and was running by the time I could come to a complete stop.

I exited my vehicle, identified myself and called to him by name to stop so I could talk to him. I wasn't sure he knew of the warrant but it didn't matter. He was gone. I was able to follow him on foot staying pretty close for about two blocks then he turned between two houses, one of which I thought was his. The area between the houses was unimproved dirt that was now of course just mud.

As he was well into the slippery mess I turned the corner ordering him to halt again. I felt it wise to draw my revolver, a Smith and Wesson Model 28 .357 with a four inch barrel. While drawing, I again order him to stop but to no avail. As this was going on I lost my footing in the mud and to prevent falling down I was able to keep from falling into the muddy mire but while doing so I extended the muzzle of my revolver into the mud.

I feared the worse and a quick glance showed me that I now had an obstructed barrel meaning my revolver was of no use to me. I certainly didn't want to bluff someone with a firearm that would not fire, at least without it blowing up. I continued to the rear corner of the house and he was nowhere in sight with many options to him to continue his flight. My common sense finally kicked in and I retreated.

At least my report would show that an additional charge of eluding a police officer would be rendered against this subject. Allowing my revolver to become inoperable during a foot pursuit was not something I would broadcast to even my best buddies although thinking back it would have been a good learning "story" for other officers.

FOOT PURSUIT AND ARREST WITHOUT MY REVOLVER

Now to move on to another situation that was similar but had a different cause that "disarmed" me during a pursuit. Again I was patrolling my beat alone in my black and white in the downtown business area well after 2 am. Remember what I said earlier about not much happening on graveyard shift? Most of the activity from the closing of the bars and restaurants was pretty much over. But being a business area it was also a very common location for burglaries.

The patrols and business checks kept us busy during graveyard shift as we never wanted a burglary reported to the department when an owner or employee showed up to work to start the next business day. At least we wanted to make the discovery if not an arrest. I always had a pair of binoculars and a hand held spotlight with me and when traffic became light or non- existent I patrolled five m.p.h. or slower without vehicle lights. We also made physical checks of doors and windows. But a downside to this was when we were out of our patrol car we didn't have any method of communication.

This particular early morning, when I turned from a street into an alley that ran between two businesses I saw a subject run across the far end of the alley carrying something. I accelerated and drove to the end of the alley and saw the subject I could now identify only as a white adult male. He ran to a wooden fence, dropped the box which turned out to contain stolen items obtained during his break-in at one of the nearby businesses then climbed over the eight to ten foot high fence. I drove to the fence, exited my vehicle, climbed the fence behind him and dropped to the other side from the top. Adrenaline was of course pumping so I didn't notice any adverse effects after jumping from the top of the fence. I was pumped and being young and healthy felt no pain and was able to catch, subdue and arrest the subject after a fifty to seventy-five yard chase.

After cuffing and searching him, I walked him around to where my vehicle was and placed him in the secure back seat. I picked up the box that contained miscellaneous electronic equipment, obvious fruits of his crime, and transported him to the station for booking.

Soon after arrival I noticed that something was missing from my belt. I discovered that my revolver and holster were gone. The holster that I was wearing on my duty belt was a leather "western" type black basket weave holster that hung down from my belt on my strong or gun side. It was attached to the belt portion of the leather by a metal swivel. That was what broke, most likely as I landed on the far side of the fence.

One would think that it would be obvious that this happened when it did but it was not the case that night. As soon as the prisoner was secured in our holding cell I returned to the fence and sure enough the holster and revolver were on the ground right where I had landed from the top of the fence.

Guess who went to a different style holster? Not the real security type but at least a high ride with no breakable swivels was my choice. This worked until many new and revolutionary holsters were developed and made available.

Just to complete the details of this case, I returned to the office and completed my crime and arrest reports. As soon as I got up from the desk I didn't feel so young and healthy. My landing on the ground from the top of the fence apparently caused a strain in my lower back but thankfully it bothered me for only a few days or so and was not something that I considered serious enough to be a reportable as an "on the job injury". A side note here; as I write this I am seeing a neurosurgeon and pain management doctor for a problem with my lower right back. Who knows?

MY FIGHT TO CONTROL MY HOLSTERED REVOLVER

Some of the safety and security procedures that are common practice today hadn't been identified as being necessary when I was a police officer. A great example is this next experience that I lived through with help from "above". I still thank my God for watching over me as He continues to do so today. We had a separate booking room just prior to the hall with the jail cells. This was where we got the necessary prisoner information including fingerprints, photographs and other booking information. We had a cell block that also had a "padded" cell and a separate cell for those who needed time to sober up.

One very important place or facility that we did not have was a locker or other secure storage place for our side-arms. We entered our jail facility fully armed all the time.

Very early one morning I brought a prisoner in to process and place in a cell that was no big deal, just a "routine" procedure, right? He was not a felon and had no history of violence with our department but he was unknown to us.

He and I had casual conversation as I removed the handcuffs from his wrists, all was well. While I was getting the forms out to complete during booking he attacked me. His left arm went around my upper body and with his right hand he grabbed my holstered revolver. As I explained in an earlier situation we didn't have the security type holsters that are in use today. I placed both my hands over his hand not allowing his hand to remove my revolver. We fought in this position a short time until I was able to get him down and bend his fingers enough to make him release his grip. A fellow officer in the break room heard the commotion and responded as I was re-cuffing him. This additional charge of assaulting a police officer added to his booking sheet turned out to be the most serious offense considered by the court.

From that night on I became acutely aware of the location of my side-arm whether carrying open or concealed. My strong side which is also my gun side is always the side of my stance that is away from a suspect or anybody I am speaking with. Even today I am more comfortable in this position while talking to anybody. This is referred to as the bladed stance, interrogation stance or self defense stance. This is one of the first things taught now. Also I should have been aware of his proximity to me and I'm sure he was studying or at least looking at my revolver and holster before he acted.

VEHICLE PURSUIT – 130 MPH

Here I will tell you about my longest and fastest vehicle pursuit that concluded with a foot pursuit and ended with one in custody. Again on graveyard shift where a normal, or did I mean to say routine patrol had been quiet with no activity reported from dispatch. I found it was a good night to have with me a young fifteen year old high school student who was a member of our department sponsored explorer scout troop. These were teens from fifteen to eight-teen years old who were interested in pursuing a law enforcement career.

During their training with us they started with office work and continued with other areas of training. When they became proficient in all the training subjects they were considered for "ride-a-longs" where they accompanied an officer on patrol during his shift. Before they would be released to patrol with an officer, they had to be well versed in our "10" code and protocol for radio communications.

They were also taught about cover and concealment and other tactical considerations but most of all they needed to know how to take orders from their companion officer without hesitation or question. The only equipment they carried was a set of handcuffs as an extra set for their officer if needed. I had this same young man with me on previous patrols so I knew his capabilities and his desire to do well and learn all about police work. So we checked out our vehicle, my favorite black and white, and readied our equipment for patrol.

Like I mentioned it was a quiet week night and I was assigned the downtown patrol area. We had three designated patrol areas and usually had an officer assigned to each beat with the shift sergeant assisting and monitoring all city activity. The bars and restaurants had closed with nothing out of the ordinary happening. We slowly drove the main business areas and checked the alleys for activity or unusual or out of place vehicles.

When you worked a designated area for a three month period you became familiar with lights, vehicles and the few businesses that had employees leaving late or arriving early preparing for the next business day. As I turned onto one of the main streets that headed out of town, I saw a vehicle that was familiar to me a few blocks away. When I got close enough to make a positive identification my suspicion was confirmed. I had made prior contact with the same vehicle and owner and was aware of outstanding felony warrants for the owner. I can still to this day remember the vehicle, make, model and license number and of course the name of the owner and driver.

I advised my sergeant and dispatch of my observation and where I would be making the stop. My sergeant acknowledged my call and told me he was en-route. I activated my red light and pulled the suspect vehicle over. He complied with no hesitation. I approached and confirmed his identity asking a few general questions regarding his activities being out this early in the morning.

My sergeant approached in his vehicle from the opposite direction and stopped directly across from us as I was talking to the suspect. I had arrested this subject before for lesser offenses and he was always compliant. When I asked to see his driver's license he responded by putting his vehicle in gear and accelerating forward with the maximum speed his vehicle would do. I was in a safe position while conversing with him so did not sustain any injuries.

I immediately ran back to my vehicle, got in and told my explorer scout "ride-a-long" to maintain radio contact with my sergeant and dispatch informing them of all that was happening as we took up the chase. He was fantastic throughout the next fifteen minutes. I heard him as he spoke clearly transmitting the necessary information. I didn't have to tell him what to say. That was a tremendous help as we accelerated to 130 m.p.h. on the straight two lane road. My sergeant was the "pace car" as I didn't bother with the speedometer just the concentration required during this high speed chase.

After a few miles we left the city limits and entered into an unincorporated area that had scattered businesses and houses with large open fields in between. Luckily we encountered no other traffic on this two lane roadway so I was able to maintain a good visual on him even as he had his lights off as we continued on the fairly straight roadway. After a few more miles he suddenly turned left and drove across the opposing traffic lane, over the road shoulder and out into an open field with low vegetation and dips and gullies.

His vehicle was altered to make it fit in with the current trend by being lowered which was really cool but this obviously decreased its' ground clearance. After crossing over a few acres of this rough terrain, I got lucky as he high centered and lost traction and came to a sudden stop. His vehicle stopped but he didn't and now a foot pursuit continued. Knowing that my commands for him to "stop" would not be obeyed at this point a foot chase was the only option.

I had played two years of junior college football prior to my military service where I won the trophy for high score in the obstacle course and now a few years later still in pretty good physical condition. This helped as I was able to catch up to him during the foot chase, tackle him and take him into custody. Only one other person witnessed this conclusion, my explorer scout companion. My sergeant was there immediately but the radio broadcast of, "one in custody – code 4" came from my "ride-a-long" that memorable early morning.

ATTEMPTED RAPIST ARRESTED

This situation ended in a short foot pursuit and was one that I was so thankful that I was in the right place at the right time. My graveyard shift had been uneventful, a very quiet week night that was coming to an end. The bars were closed and activity was limited. The downtown restaurants were closing up and vehicle traffic had just about cleared from the downtown business area.

I spent some time parked on side streets where I could see and listen for activity. Shortly after 2:00 a.m. I began cruising very slow with lights out and windows open as I often did on these quiet nights. Our business area had side and rear alleys that were drivable but also good areas for hiding if someone was up to no good. There were large cardboard boxes from television and electronic stores and packing boxes from furniture stores mixed in with the other trash that didn't find its' way into the dumpsters.

It was approaching 3:00 a.m. and the only traffic was the employees of the bars and restaurants that were now on their way home. As I crept along a main street I heard a loud scream from a female. I did not see anyone so kept going in the same direction toward a large parking lot. I called an officer for assistance then I heard a scream again but this time it was a loud cry for "help!"

When I turned into the parking lot I saw a man on top of the woman who continued to scream. Her screams for help must have covered any noise that my vehicle made. She was on her back and he was on top of her. Some of her outer clothing had been torn and her dress was up around her waist. I got out of my patrol car and with gun drawn ran toward them. He saw me, got up and started running to the far end of the parking lot. When I got to her I saw that she seemed okay considering the attack that just occurred.

I continued after him and when I got to the far side of the lot he was not in sight. But there was so much open space I thought I would be able to see him as he continued on away from me. No such luck but there was a large garbage dumpster at the far end of the lot. The lid was open so my next option was to check it out as there was no other place he could be hiding. He was there and I ordered him out at gun point then cuffed and searched him. He had no weapons. My back-up arrived, saw me, remember no portable radios, and I transferred custody to him.

I returned to the victim who was now standing at my patrol vehicle. She said that she did not know him. She just got off work as a waitress and was walking to her vehicle when he suddenly attacked her. She told me she was not raped but that his intentions were clear. He had no weapons but he easily overpowered her. She was very thankful for my timely appearance. She declined medical care and no injuries were apparent so we went to the department for additional investigation and reports. The victim was a local waitress in her mid thirties and the suspect was a minor under eighteen although he was 6'1 and about 170 pounds. I thanked the Lord for my timely arrival to the scene. Sometimes situations work out for the best.

RESPONSE TO SHOTS FIRED DOWNTOWN

This incident turned out to be unusual, kind of like something from the old west. Shots heard in the downtown area were not unusual especially at night. But this is an incident that isn't heard of much, "a shoot-out on Main Street". I guess it illustrates that anything can happen on the streets of a busy urban area. I was the first officer to arrive at the scene of my downtown patrol area in response to the report of shots fired on a main street of a particularly busy area where lots of shopping took place and in the middle of the day.

Upon arriving in the area, I parked on a side street and made my approach on foot hoping to see what was happening from a safe vantage point. A very excited woman came up to me right away and told me that two women that she didn't know were shooting at each other from opposite sidewalks of the main street and that each had fired at least two times. In fact as she was talking I heard two more gun shots. I advised dispatch and the other responding officer of this additional information. I thanked the woman and told her I would like to talk to her later for additional information and advised her where she should go to be safe.

When the other officer arrived he took a side street approach as I did but on the other side of the street and a block down from me. It was obvious who the shooters were and they were contained between us. Fortunately the shoppers and others on the street understood the seriousness of the situation and thankfully had disappeared into the stores without having to be told to take cover. I watched as the other officer took his position. We had no portable radios in those days so the ever important hand signals were put to use.

I kept close against each store wall as I each inched my way toward the shooter on my side of the street using the store entry ways as my only cover from incoming shots. When close enough and before they decided to shoot again I shouted, "Police, don't move, put your guns on the ground!" I heard similar commands from the other officer.

The two women were both white and in their late thirty's. They had blonde hair and were dressed more for partying than gun fighting as if they had just left one of the local bars. They responded immediately by putting their guns on the sidewalk. They did not try to flee but they continuing shouting profanities at each other blaming the other for their actions. We approached them, secured the .38 caliber revolvers, and placed them under arrest. A quick survey of the area did not reveal any injuries or damage.

We kept them separate and transported them to the department for questioning and booking. Keeping them separated as they were questioned about their deadly confrontation, we learned of some of the details of their dispute that was evidently a product of their jealously over a boyfriend. This was apparently an ongoing battle that they decided to settle once and for all. As you can imagine alcohol also played a part in their actions on this day.

A minimal charge was brought against them for discharging a firearm in the city limits, as neither desired to press charges against the other for assault with a deadly weapon. I'm sure they thought they could settle their ongoing differences later hopefully by using other means. As soon as possible the other officer and me returned to the scene to again determine if there were any injuries we were unaware of. Amazingly, no property damage was reported or found. They each paid a fine and forfeited their revolvers.

A BUSY AND DANGEROUS CHRISTMAS EVE

This happened on Christmas Eve and could have been the final response for my partner and I, it was that close. As described in previous incidents, gun fire had become pretty common in the downtown area of our community and some resulted in victims either injured or with fatal wounds.

"Shots fired inside a downtown bar" was the report relayed to on duty officers by our dispatcher. It was late that night so I knew that alcohol was most likely a consideration. I and one other officer were the only one's available for response. Instead of providing additional officers to work on Christmas Eve it was policy to allow officers the option to be at home for the holiday but actually it went by seniority. I was the first one to arrive at this bar that was popular for locals as well as visitors from neighboring cities.

There was a group gathered just outside the front door and I was met by some very excited older patrons and was told that a woman had been shot several times and was still in the bar. I could not determine any information about a shooter, again due to the excitement and inebriation of the group so I cautiously entered to locate an injured person to see if the reports were true.

Upon entry, I noticed that the bar stools were all unoccupied except for one and that one was occupied by a very large white woman that appeared to be forty five or fifty years old. I estimated her weight at 300 pounds. She sat with a partially consumed drink in one hand and did not appear to be in any distress. Someone shouted to me "she's been shot"! and indicated the woman at the bar.

As I cautiously approached her I was still trying to identify a shooter who may still be in the bar area. Seeing that no one appeared suspicious I contacted her. I noticed some small red stains on her dress located at her hip area. She was very drunk and couldn't give me any information but indicated that she was okay and would remain on the bar stool. I didn't know how she was able to remain seated but now I was more concerned about who had done the shooting. Still no information was forthcoming regarding a shooter.

I then went outside to radio the other responding officer and dispatch to advise them of what I knew of the situation at that time. I requested an ambulance and my partner advised me that he was just about at the bar. He parked alongside my vehicle then met me on the sidewalk just outside the front door of the bar.

As I was giving him the details as I presently knew them, the bar doors opened and two male Hispanic adults who were strangers to us exited to the side walk and continued toward us. I immediately saw that one of them had a fixed blade hunting type knife in one hand. It had a six inch blade. He came toward me and was so close and fearing for my life and not having time to draw my sidearm I engaged him with the intent of disarming him. We struggled with me concentrating on the knife hand and arm and I was able to get the knife from him. Just as I did I observed the approach of the other man toward my partner. He had a pistol in his hand and had it pointed at my partners head. They also were within reach of each other.

We both heard the hammer fall as this man pulled the trigger. The pistol did not fire and gave my partner the second he needed to disarm him of his pistol. God had to be there that night to save us each from receiving serious or fatal wounds. We took both men into custody without further incident.

It was unknown at this point what the motive had been but given the racial difference between the suspect's and victim one could wonder if that was a factor. The suspects would not or could not speak to a motive or reason for their actions but they knew how to engage a defense attorney the next day. The reason why the pistol did not fire? We later found out that the two men had retreated to the rear restroom area of the bar just after the shooting. When apparently reloading with the action closed and without using the slide to re-chamber a bullet the pistol was not loaded. By pulling the hammer back and releasing it with the trigger would not chamber a round so it would not fire.

The woman victim at the bar was found to have four entry wounds from the .45 caliber semi-auto pistol, none of which exited. Her large body seemed to have absorbed the bullets enough to keep them from striking vital areas. A very good reason to pack around a few extra pounds I guess, especially in her case. She did survive and I imagine she found comfort once again in that same place and on that same bar stool. Must have been where she was during the trial as she nor any others would testify against them.

At the trial, their defense attorney made the case for "deportation" instead of jail or prison time as they were not citizens. There was some credit for time served but as for their future endeavors one can only guess. As far as the attempted murder of police officers, no big deal.

MOLOTOV COCKTAILS VS PATROL VEHICLE

How about another "ride-along" with you tonight? asked the explorer scout who had accompanied me on patrol several times. "No school tomorrow so I can do the whole swing shift with you. I was able to get some rest before reporting in tonight" he said. "Sure", I told him. He was always eager and ready to learn more about police work and I always enjoyed his company and in some cases assistance.

This was the same young man that was with me during the 130 m.p.h. vehicle chase that ended with a foot pursuit and arrest that I described earlier. This shift turned out to be a pretty active. A busy Friday night with an on duty force of three officers and one sergeant. As the night progressed or better put, "regressed", more officers were called in to work. Social unrest was on the upswing that night and through the weekend.

Our city was divided into three sectors with one officer assigned to each. We backed each other up as we could but sometimes we were all handling a call. By nature, the 4:00 p.m. to 12:00 a.m. shift was busier than graveyard which is understandable considering many more people were moving around the streets; shopping, dining, drinking and some just out to have fun and others out to see that those same people didn't have fun. Heroin and cocaine were the drugs of choice but marijuana, hashish, LSD and a mix of pills and capsules were also common.

Our downtown area had some very popular card rooms that even drew players from surrounding communities. Not only was gambling a draw but "ladies of the night" were also on the prowl and available at the Clubs. An "outlaw" motorcycle group, the most popular group during this period, also had ties to our city because of resident members and proximity to one of its' main hangouts. It was not unusual to see fifteen to twenty bikers enter our city for their "recreational" activities but sometimes also came rival gangs that added to the "fun".

We were also dealing with racial unrest that had spread throughout most of the large interracial cities in the nation at this time. Although we were not one of the largest cities in the area we still felt the tension and had to deal with the resultant criminal activity. "Mutual Aid" was a great way for communities to obtain assistance from their brothers from surrounding jurisdictions. Requests for assistance were fairly common during this period.

We had a different philosophy about patrol during swing shift as opposed to graveyard shift. We wanted to be seen in as many places as reasonably possible during swing shift to give the appearance of a well patrolled city in hopes that some illegal or criminal activity would be thwarted. This did not mean racing from place to place but a purposeful patrol of the areas where most of the crime has occurred in the past. On graveyard shift as I had indicated before we wanted to see the illegal activity and criminals before they saw us.

Toward the end of this particular shift I got a radio dispatch to respond to a small grocery store that was located at the edge of town in a black residential area. The owner reported that a group of local kids and young adults stole some things while in his store and when he confronted them as they left they began throwing rocks, cans and bottles at him and at the windows in front of the store breaking some of the large ones.

When I arrived the group of dissidents, fifty to sixty, had retreated to the parking lot alongside the store. I did not intend to exit my patrol vehicle but wanted to break up their "party". I used the public address system to advise the group to break-up and leave the area. Just as I did this my vehicle was pelted with bottles, cans and rocks thrown by the departing crowd.

No real damage was done, but we then became lit up with fire that surrounded our vehicle. Flames extended up both sides visible from both side windows. Molotov cocktails, at least two, had been thrown at us. My engine was still running so I immediately drove from the parking lot and exited the area. I stopped and checked for fire damage and to see if there was anything burning and all seemed OK.

Back-up arrived but all was now quiet. We were then available to go to the downtown area and support the other officers who were dealing with some unruly gang activity.

The store owner was able to identify some in the crowd but couldn't say who caused the damage. This store was one of the first in our city to install iron bars over all windows and doors. The vehicle was checked by our city mechanics and no serious damage was detected, just some paint melting and peeling and some dents. Apparently the flare up from the Molotov Cocktails was quick enough that there was no major fire or flame damage.

CHAPTER 7

UNIFORM VERSUS
UNDERCOVER PATROL

I include this chapter to describe to you some of the uniform, vehicle and equipment considerations that became important to me during my early career as a police officer and then during my years as a game warden. Some of the investigations described in the following chapters were conducted undercover or at least out of uniform and my "non-enforcement" appearance that was meant to blend in with the surrounding area and activities played a major role in creating a successful outcome for many of the investigative stages of cases described.

During my police officer years I began as a uniformed officer patrolling in a marked police vehicle in those days referred to as a "black and white" and that's what it was. My assigned car was car number eight and had a red spotlight located in the driver side door jamb. No fancy light bars but just red and yellow lights in the rear window or in the case of our canine station wagons a light bar was across the roof.

The equipment available to me and to all officers during the beginning of my police work was so different than what is available and required to carry today. We bought our own uniforms but were issued helmets that had to be worn at all times when outside and in the patrol vehicle. We had no other headgear they were just part of our everyday uniform.

Our department developed a SWAT team that was necessary during the riotous times of the late sixties. We again had to purchase our own military fatigue uniforms for this use. Our training was conducted by an active military sniper/trainer. His experience, plus his knowledge of our role in these special situations was also very important and a very necessary catalyst in our team's development. We were also on call to respond to "mutual aid" requests by neighboring cities or counties. Our team was even called to assist at a city fifty miles away which was experiencing serious civil unrest and is even requiring police action for demonstrations as I write this.

Of course when I was promoted to detective I was out of uniform except for times when our SWAT team was called upon for a response. Although not directly assigned to the narcotics enforcement division I was also called upon to assist when additional bodies were needed during surveillance, actual residential or business raids, or service of search warrants. My personal pick-up and camper was utilized for stakeouts of suspects' homes or businesses. I parked it where the officer in back would have a good view then I would walk away and get picked up around the corner. Thinking back, I may have failed to include this activity on my insurance coverage.

Working for the state wildlife agency was somewhat different. Game wardens could be highly visible one minute but as an investigation or situation dictated we may want to be just another hunter, fisherman or tourist the next minute. Similar to the additional training we received while on the SWAT team of the police department we also secured an active duty military trainer to provide our squad with cover, concealment, movement during night and day and night tactics including training with night vision optics. He helped us to become invisible and but still able to observe activity from a concealed location.

I was led to understand this facet of the job my first day as a game warden when I reported to the regional office of the patrol district I was assigned. I was issued three things; my badge, a pair of binoculars and directions to my assigned patrol district about 250 miles away. I still have this initial set of Bushnell binoculars and they are my choice for hunting to this day, inexpensive, light weight and easy to use.

Upon arrival at my first assigned district, I was issued my patrol vehicle, a Plymouth sedan that was raised for clearance to get around on some of the back roads. In the trunk was a box containing radiological equipment, a "Geiger Counter" with a handbook and student workbook. I got the message that we were also "Radiological Monitors". Then as I received more of the equipment assigned to me, the nature of the job was reinforced with the addition of a variable power spotting scope. I mounted this on a rifle stock and as I got used to it I found that I depended on it for surveillance much more than the binoculars.

During my first years as a fish and game warden our state was converting from sedans to four-wheel drive pick-ups. When I got to my second fish and game station I was issued another sedan, a matador, with low mileage so in order to get to remote areas in this my second patrol district, I got a Honda 90 trail bike that I mounted on a rack I had installed across the rear bumper. I made this work but not without frequent body work along the lower panels and fenders.

Several months later I was able to have a conversation with our director during a "meeting-fly fishing-campout" in the back country. He heard my plea and shortly thereafter my sedan was replaced with a new four-wheel drive pick-up.

Additionally, and I think I can speak for most wardens, we had the means to go in and out of uniform with clothing and equipment we carried with us in our patrol vehicles. This could include hunting and fishing equipment depending on the seasons and even a visible camera and sport shirt to take on the appearance of a tourist while checking a situation on foot as a situation may call for.

All wardens had access to an unmarked, normal looking vehicle usually a pick-up if needed for undercover and out of uniform patrol or investigation. I remember the first "undercover" vehicle I used was a twenty year old Jeep pick-up which used more oil than gasoline. Somewhat "normal" looking but a little scary considering I used it for patrols into remote mountainous areas at times when an overnight patrol was called for. Due to its age, condition and appearance I learned early on that it was not "undercover" at all but was recognized by most residents, especially fishermen, hunters and probably potential "poachers". This was indicated to me because of some early contacts when I was greeted by, "Hi, you must be the new warden". I was relieved when the department saw fit to replace it shortly after I arrived.

With the different unmarked pick-ups we used, a good friend from the forest service had a large magnetic sticker made for each door that described a fictitious business. I knew this additional means of disguise was noticed as one day a man called my attention to the "business license number". Our state issued a six-digit business number and the number I had for the fake business name had only five-digits. So that was easy to change.

In the list of training subjects back in the first chapter you most likely noticed training in many different modes of transportation while on patrol. Certain times of the year prompted us to use snowshoes, skis and snowmobiles so we had to have training in their use as well as cold weather survival and snow camping.

The summer months meant patrols to high elevations and in areas where backpacking and horse patrol were the only means of access. Our first thought would be, "wow, that sounds like fun and getting paid too?" Well, don't be fooled. I found that a normal horse patrol day in the backcountry was about fourteen hours.

First thing was to break camp, then get the horses and

mules fed, equipped and ready with blanket, saddle and bridle, etc. and then at the end of the day the last thing was to feed and put them to "bed" meaning tying them to a "high line". Of course setting up another camp, and cooking a meal was the end of the day. The actual "horse patrol" was okay once the soreness wore off. I almost had to learn to walk again after a four day horse patrol. That's just a quick description. It was really much easier to backpack into the remote areas where one could travel cross country and not have to depend on established trails. Had to be in shape though but it was worth it to me.

Some other patrols that required uncomfortable "campouts" due to distance from my home or having to be at a certain location before hunting hours or maybe an unexpected night out were fairly frequent. Campfires and cooking meals was never a part of these campouts so I was a fan of tuna, spam, cheese and crackers and this menu even remains a great meal source for me when hunting and fishing to this day.

The most uncomfortable place I camped was a high desert location during quail and chukar season. Seventy five miles to the beginning of a very rocky and washed out "vehicle trail". I can't call it a road and was always so glad when I got back to the blacktop the next day. The presence of rattlesnakes was the other problem. I saw at least one large diamondback every time I was in this area and smaller sidewinders as well. Seeing them active any time night or day was the issue so I made my bed on top of the toolbox across my truck bed immediately behind the rear window. This was not the most comfortable bed but I felt it was the safest.

The next most uncomfortable camping location was during backpack trips to the high country. It was well above the timber line and mostly consisted of sand and boulders. Some of the lakes found in the high mountains produced some really good fishing and were popular. Camping was not so good though. First traveling light meant that the bare minimum equipment and bedding was carried. Curling up in the sand between boulders was secure and provided protection from wind if needed. The nights were very bright in this environment due to the stars and possibly the moon, just ambient light.

Another warden and I planned a patrol with a different twist. We would be on foot in order to watch deer hunters who were on horseback. We made many high country foot patrols together but mainly during the summer months and for illegal fishing activity.

This particular patrol was in November to target illegal deer hunters. The situation was our deer season was closed but the season in a neighboring county was open. We had knowledge that hunters would indicate they were going to the next county but they would hunt way short of the county line especially if the weather got rough.

A few more facts: the county line was just over 11,000 feet in elevation and any moisture would be snow and there was a probability of stormy weather. Our hike from the trailhead was about ten miles. We were dropped off at the trailhead by another warden early one Friday morning so we would have no vehicle in the parking lot. No other vehicles were parked at this time so we were going to get a "step" ahead of any hunters.

We kept our packs light with enough stuff for two days and one overnight. We brought no hunting equipment as we planned to remain out of sight while watching for any activity. We carried with us a newly issued portable radio just in case. We hiked to a spot to set up our tent which was the extent of our "camp" that would be out of sight from hunters or anyone else who may be on the trail. The wind was picking up as we found a vantage point behind a line of thick brush. A short walk from our tent put us where we could watch a section of the trail for any activity. All was going as planned as we watched but no activity was seen or heard.

As it got to be mid afternoon the cloud cover became heavier and lower and the temperature dropped. We saw the first hunters on horseback heading up the trail to the county line. They had two pack mules with them. Through my binoculars I recognized the two men from town and would not suspect them of illegal hunting and was sure that they were heading over the pass to camp and hunt legally in the next county. Another lone hunter passed on the trail a little later also heading up to the county line and to country that was open to deer hunting. I also knew him from good contacts in the past.

Darkness came upon us along with increasing wind, snow and still lowering temperatures. We were now in camp with the idea of boiling some water to heat some "top ramen", our main course. My tent had a separate rain fly that protected the screened ridge of the main tent body from rain or snow so I thought. The horizontal wind blew the snow between the layers where it then blew into the tent and rapidly began covering our sleeping bags. We made some adjustments that helped but we had to work to keep the tent itself in tact as the cold wind continued to increase.

We knew it was getting colder attested by my inability to heat the water on my backpack stove. In fact the water froze while on the flame! We had some other food that didn't need cooking so that wasn't the issue. We got so cold that we felt the first stages of hypothermia. We continued to get colder and decided to pack up and head for lower ground. We departed hiking down the trail toward the trailhead. The temperature remained cold and the wind and snow continued to follow us all the way. Once at the trailhead at about 11:30 p.m. we were able to call for a ride home.

CHAPTER 8

LESSONS LEARNED
FROM CONTACTS

Some situations helped me to realize that strange and unexpected things can and do happen and at any time. At the time when making initial contact with suspect(s) and at the beginning of most investigations I developed awareness that the suspect(s) may take flight either by vehicle, foot or both. Another possibility could be by boat although I never experienced a boat pursuit as the James Bond movies so "realistically" portray. I made many investigative contacts while patrolling rivers, lakes and ocean waters, in various types of patrol vessels but always seemed to get some level of cooperation from the suspects short of having them flee from me.

One thing that was a given during my law enforcement years, there was no such thing as a partner unless during a specific assignment or in some cases an undercover assignment All patrols were solo so that's usually how we arrived at a scene, by ourselves and with only the possibility of a back up officer to come to your aid in a timely manner. Some situations allowed for a brief waiting period if another officer was free and nearby but this was a rarity.

Most of the pursuits I was engaged in occurred during my time as a police officer. I think that during the course of my training and experiences and generally a maturing process, I became better at controlling the initial steps when contacting persons and suspects so that flight became less of a consideration by them. Verbal Judo classes presented to our fish and game department by the late George Thompson later in my career were a vital part of my success in conducting interviews and interrogations but probably most importantly the verbal skills that he taught became the first tools I used during almost all contacts. During his classes we learned how to "redirect a person's behavior with words". He also stressed that to "be good" you had to "look good" and "sound good". I took this training very seriously and even now have used it to assist our "Shepherd" security group in church to carry out our mission to "watch over our flock" especially before, after and during worship services.

I began many of my contacts of suspects by telling them what I observed during my brief or lengthy surveillance period or maybe what I knew about their activities from citizen reports or other intelligence. I think perhaps my honesty with them brought out some level of honesty from them. Calling them suspects was in lots of cases a misnomer because I already knew that an offense has been committed after all I was the eye witness so they were now known violators.

It was different, though, when making a vehicle stop of someone known to have active arrest warrants especially felony warrants or when observing the same wanted individuals on foot or when contacting individuals that you have had prior contact with. When a suspect flees, an instant decision has to be made whether or not to pursue. So much has to be considered. I like to believe that all law enforcement officers are in good physical condition and required by their department to remain in good condition not only for their own safety but for the safety of those he has sworn to serve and protect.

I laud our fish and game department for initiating an annual physical program that was in effect during the last ten years of my career. It was very complete and conducted by medical professionals. It included a timed 200 yard swim, step test, lower back strength test and of course blood pressure, heart rate and cholesterol checks. Other than a reward of knowing I was in okay shape for my age we got sixty one dollars per month in addition to our regular pay. I know some agencies are pretty lax in this area just by observing some of those in uniform. The reason for this concern is that many vehicle pursuits end up being a foot pursuit or an actual physical struggle.

CHAPTER 9

FISH AND GAME WARDEN
1970-1998

WHY FISH AND GAME?

My law enforcement career was well under way but to make it complete I need the third agency in the equation. I went from federal to city now on to a state agency. Most importantly at this time in my life I was a husband and together with my wife, who also worked full time as a registered nurse in the hospital in the city where we lived were in the process of learning how to raise our first child, a daughter. We had neighbors who supported us in our occupations and helped us tremendously with babysitting and by just being great neighbors during our first few years of marriage. We still remained in contact with them but during the writing of this book both have passed away.

I always had a hunger for outdoor activities such as fishing, hunting, boating, hiking and camping, probably nurtured during my boy scout years and some of which (except for the hunting and boy scouting) was also part of my wife's prior life and interests. I knew I

picked a winner for life when
she agreed that we could go tent
camping along a river in the
mountains on our honeymoon.
I even caught us some trout for
dinner. Anyway, we would
pursue these other interests
during times we could get away

from our job responsibilities and while on vacations.

Some research into the opportunities that existed out there for me
while still wanting to remain in law enforcement, as I knew nothing
else, directed me to apply to our state wildlife agency. My prior
service with the army (veteran's preference points were added to my
test score) and my current law enforcement position as a detective in
a city police department together with my training and experience
from these prior agencies helped me to get a position with a fish and
game department as a game warden.

Having possessed the necessary law enforcement certifications
meant I was ready to assume my new duties in the same state but with
different and additional responsibilities and in a rural location. My
initial assigned location was an area with a high population of doves
and therefore during the dove season that opened every September 1,
it was very popular with hunters, most of whom drove 200 miles for
their twenty dove possession limit. I had never hunted doves before
and my first day as a game warden was the first day of the dove
season so I had a lot of learning to do and fast if I was to be effective
in enforcing the regulations. My captain supervisor and neighboring
wardens had the patience to give me the informal training necessary
that I so desperately needed.

Our department did something differently than other agencies.
We served our own warrants meaning that when a violator was cited
to appear in court and failed to appear as directed a warrant was
issued for his or her arrest. Most of our violators lived in a large
metropolitan area about 200 miles away so teams were formed to
spend a week or two away from their home assigned to a "warrant

detail". I'm sure I was always the one chosen for this detail because of my prior police experience. But that was fine.

We rendezvoused at a centrally located motel and worked in pairs attempting to contact the violators who "failed to appear" in our court. We tried to collect the fine instead of taking them into custody and would drive them to a store, bank or even a friend's house in order to collect the amount of the fine or bail. I didn't have to arrest too many over the course of three years doing this. Just like my police days though, some would exit the rear door and keep on running.

We knew that one man we were trying to contact worked and could never find him at home. We staked out his house early in the morning and waited for him to leave for work. We watched as his car would leave his garage with only a woman driving two mornings in a row. She had a bathrobe on which was a little strange so the third morning we stopped her, a block away from their home and found him on the floorboard of the rear seat. He was happy to pay his fine without having to go to jail and we were happy to end the "game".

During the early 1970's some communities were still being affected by recent "racial unrest" and rioting. One morning while staking out a house in a predominately black neighborhood a police unit drove up with two officers dressed in riot gear. They questioned our reason for being there and requested, pretty firmly, that we leave for our own protection. We learned later that we were in an area where the residents were presently exhibiting anti-police behavior.

We headed to another area of town and more into the foothills where we had another outstanding warrant to serve. Would you believe it, the house at our next stop had about ten Harleys parked in front. Yes, "Hells Angels" but they thought it was pretty funny that one of their buddies was being pursued by "fish and game". We got along pretty good, turned down a beer, collected the fine then checked the map for another fun place to go.

Its' important for me to include here some physical and health considerations and decisions that I had to make at this time of my life. Important because with an unexpected situation requiring a physical response that faces all law enforcement officers every day a successful outcome can depend on our physical conditioning and strength.

I was twenty seven when I began my twenty eight years as a fish and game warden and I found that two habits I carried forward from my prior life did not fit with the this new job. Living and working in some very different locations required me to be more focused on my physical condition and the ability to perform at a higher level. First, within my first year I gave up smoking. It was after a New Year's party and probably because I felt so crummy I made the decision to quit "cold turkey". I had smoked from college years on and tried to back off the cigarettes by using a pipe and I even changed to cigars for a short period. Anyway, quitting was something I was proud of.

My next "challenge" was to get rid of a dependence I developed to caffeine. I don't remember if they even had de-caffeinated coffee then. I liked coffee and didn't miss many coffee breaks but I found with fish and game patrols one couldn't schedule coffee breaks let alone be somewhere in the vicinity of a coffee shop when the desire or what became a need struck. I got frequent headaches and it didn't take long for me to figure out they were related to the lack of caffeine.

All was well but brought me to another problem that came on rather gradually. Weight gain, as I substituted food and fruit juice for what I missed with smokes and coffee. I always carried snacks and drinks in my patrol vehicle with me so I didn't have a need to find a store or restaurant. I gained about thirty to thirty five pounds onto my 185 pounds and began to have some heart related anomalies that I blamed on stress. My doctors' advised me otherwise and convinced me that weight loss through exercise and proper diet should be my present focus.

My wife could and would help me with the diet part but only I could do the exercise part. I started with a stationary bike and after almost a year and a pretty good weight loss result I felt compelled to increase my workout intensity to jogging, which turned into running. My heart felt good and acted right but I had to get used to the periodic muscle aches and pains as I increased my running program. So after about seven years as a game warden I considered myself a "runner".

My favorite magazine was Runner's World and I kept calendars logging my miles and progress. I still have them tucked away. I hope my kids have a big fireplace for when I'm gone.

I was told several times during the ensuing years that I developed a new "addiction", running. It was true. If I missed my every other day run and couldn't log in my distance and time I felt poorly. My shorts and running shoes were with me when on patrol so if I wasn't home for lunch I could change while in the field and take a break "on the run". I wasn't into long distances and never desired to train for a marathon but I really liked to maintain my fitness level to be able to feel good competing at the 10K level. There were several 10K races for fund raisers or to just celebrate a time of year or holiday such as the fourth of July, Thanksgiving and Hospice. I tried to average less than seven minutes per mile for the 10K's. The longest local race I liked to participate in was a ten mile race run in conjunction with a marathon. The high point of this race was at 6,200 feet in elevation but lots of my everyday or training runs were done at 5,000 to 7,000 feet plus. Our department participated in a law enforcement relay race called Baker to Vegas that consisted of twenty runners over a one-hundred and twenty mile course. About one-hundred and fifty teams competed including teams from the FBI, Border Patrol, Customs, Secret Service, DEA and many other law enforcement agencies from across America and even a team from the Royal Canadian Mounted Police. We were the only group of officers from a wildlife agency that competed during the four years I was part of it, and I was over fifty years old for three of those four years. Not too bad considering the average age of our twenty runners was over forty years.

CHAPTER 10

ASSISTANCE WITH
OTHER AGENCIES

Assistance received from other agencies and being able to render assistance if needed to other agencies was very important to me and to others, I'm sure. Having a rapport with the men and women from other agencies on and off duty helped to develop a bond not only of friendship but of mutual on the job support.  This was especially helpful to me during my game warden years when we worked alone and in remote areas. I worked and trained with members of the local police, sheriff and highway patrol agencies as well as the forest service, bureau of land management, and park service.

Other than the assistance rendered in enforcing the marijuana and narcotics laws discussed in a separate chapter, I will illustrate here some other cases or instances where assistance was helpful if not depended on. We had an Incident Report Form that we were required to use to document certain situations as shown here. I completed many of these reports during my career. Note the terminology, "unusual or non-routine".

INCIDENT REPORT

This report is to be made out in the event you encounter any <u>unusual</u> or <u>non-routine</u> job related incident that may be newsworthy or documentary as to risks and hazards involved in fish and game law enforcement work, such as the following:

1. **An injury or accident sustained while effecting or assisting in an arrest if off assigned duty.**
2. **An unusual or important case or investigation.**
3. **Cases involving resistance of arrest or evasion of arrest.**
4. **Cases involving assistance to other agencies.**
5. **Cases where damage is done to sportsmen's equipment which may result in a law suit or public relations problem.**
6. **An act that was above and beyond the call of duty.**

INTO SNOW COUNTRY ON MY TRAILBIKE

While patrolling on a state highway west of town late on a Saturday afternoon I encountered a motorcyclist leaving a closed area. It was early spring and the upper portion of this highway was still closed for the winter indicated by signs and a locked gate. This "snow closure" was necessary each year due to the usual amount of snow that created public safety issues on the roadway. Plus there were privately owned buildings and summer businesses that were vacant over the winter months that could be easy targets for theft or malicious mischief.

As I approached the gate a young man on a motorcycle approached me from behind the locked gate. He came from the direction of a resort that was closed for the season and unattended. He drove around the locked gate and came toward me. I motioned for him to stop even using my red light. When he was adjacent to me and at a distance of only five feet I shouted for him to stop. He looked directly at me and immediately accelerated past me down the highway.

I turned around and pursued him with red light and siren. He was driving an off-road type motorcycle that had no visible license plate. Two miles down he turned up a county road then went another two miles to another "snow closure" gate. He also went around this gate and drove up an old mine road that was not passable by full size vehicles. I knew he would be stopped by snow when he got to the higher country as we were at 8,000 feet where he started. I called for assistance and a deputy sheriff responded from town and met me at the gate.

While I was waiting for the deputy I unloaded my state issued trail bike from the bed of my patrol truck and made preparations to continue the pursuit. With the deputy standing by I followed his track about four and a half miles to where he headed cross country  and into a snowdrift. He obviously got struck in the deep drift and fell or was thrown from his motorcycle.

He was unsuccessful with his attempt to hide his motorcycle, helmet and gloves under a tree nearby. His motorcycle was lying on its' side hidden from view from the mine road. I tracked him fifty feet to a large tree where he was attempting to hide from me. I identified myself, and after ordering him two times to come out and come to my location he complied. I searched him and gave him the Miranda warning. When I asked why he ran from me he stated that he thought I was going to cite him for being behind the snow closure gate. Well, he was right and now he will be arrested for that as well as evading an officer.

I allowed him to proceed back down to the county road on his motorcycle by maintaining a slow speed directly in front of me. We arrived back at the county road where the deputy was waiting for us. Two hours from start to finish, at least for me. He had some time to go yet.

He was placed under arrest by the deputy for; reckless driving, failing to yield to an emergency vehicle and operation of an unlicensed motor vehicle on a public roadway. His motorcycle was secured by an acquaintance of mine and owner of a lodge located at the gate area. He was transported to the county jail where he posted bail and was given a court appearance date.

I then went back to the state highway, opened the gate and drove to the area of the closed resort. I found no evidence of break-in or damage.

RESPONSE TO A TOUR-BUS ACCIDENT

Wardens' homes were our offices, with a state paid phone and safe, secure parking for our patrol vehicle and other miscellaneous storage. We had an official office in town where we met with supervisors, attended meetings, stored evidence and received miscellaneous information from dispatch. I was in the office late on a Friday morning when a call came to the office requesting assistance by all available agencies to respond to a serious bus accident at the bottom of a steep grade near a small town fifteen miles south of us.

I immediately rolled "code-3" and was one of the first responders on scene. I was thankful there were emergency medical units from the fire station nearby already on scene checking the injured. The bus was the only vehicle involved and was a tour bus full of older men and women who were tourists from a few different European countries. I assisted helping those who were the least injured exit the bus to a safe area. The bus was completely off the roadway but was still upright. The entire left side was heavily damaged including most of the windows being broken in. It scraped the rock wall on the left road shoulder then ran across the road and off the right shoulder where it sat at a fairly steep angle. Some of the more seriously injured were being tended to and being readied for transport to our hospital.

I made contact with the "tour guide" who was only slightly injured. I didn't know her nationality but she was pretty young and spoke fluent English. She had in her possession all the documentation including visas, passports, etc. of the passengers and asked if she could get a ride to the hospital so she could act as an interpreter and be able to provide information on each patient when required. Those in charge thought it was an important request so we got to my truck and left the scene for the hospital.

When at the hospital I saw my wife who obviously had her hands full assisting with triage of incoming accident victims.

There was one fatality and forty five injuries. The driver and some of the passengers stated that brake failure was the reason for the loss of control and subsequent accident. It could have been much more serious especially if there had been oncoming traffic.

ASSIST WHEN WILDLIFE VIOLATIONS ARE OBSERVED

It didn't take long for me to figure out one of the reasons why I was called by other agencies to assist as backup or with an ongoing investigation. When police officers or county deputies had reason to contact suspects in their homes, other out buildings or vehicles it was not uncommon for them to see evidence of a fish and game violation. Having a game warden to assist them freed them to deal with their primary reason for being there but another reason became clear.

While their case may involve drugs, narcotics or stolen articles, evidence they saw that involved the illegal take or possession of wildlife could be turned over to an assisting warden for further investigation. It was also known by most of us that some wildlife violations brought heavier fines or penalties than that rendered by the courts to their arrestees

ILLEGAL USE OF SPOTLIGHT

Here is a report concerning a 1:00 a.m. Saturday morning wake-up call to me by a deputy sheriff who was patrolling about eight miles south of town. From his position on the main highway he could see bright lights being shined from a moving vehicle along a parallel rural road. The deputy knew of the poaching history of this area because of the winter deer concentration.

The deputy turned off onto a cross road toward the road being travelled by the spot lighter in an attempt to make contact. When the suspect(s) saw the sheriff's car the driver turned off his vehicle lights and left the road into the brush to evade the deputy. The suspect vehicle was obviously a high clearance 4-wheel drive pick-up.

I arrived about thirty minutes later and by then there were two additional sheriff's units securing the area. I proceeded to check the area where the suspects were last seen. I located the 4X4 pick-up and it was unoccupied. A .22 rifle was in the rack along the rear window and a 12 volt spotlight was plugged into the cigarette lighter and lying on the floor were some empty .22 shell casings and also some live rounds were in the cab.

I located the subjects, both known to me, on foot nearby. We returned to the truck now in the presence of the deputies. They denied hunting animals and there was no evidence of animals observed. They both knew the violation was "shining a spot light into the fields and forests from a moving vehicle on a public roadway while possessing a firearm." So there wasn't much to talk about. I cited them and seized the spotlight and rifle as evidence. The deputies always liked to assist us as they never know what they might find of interest to them such as intoxicated drivers or hunters or possession of prohibited substances.

They both appeared in court three weeks later and pled guilty paying $190 in fines. The evidence was returned to them.

A NIGHT HUNTING CLUB WITH MULTIPLE VIOLATIONS

Another "wake-up" call this time at 3:30 a.m. again on a Saturday morning and again by a deputy sheriff who observed spot lighting from a moving vehicle on a public roadway.

Prior to my arrival he already had the pick-up stopped. When I arrived two men were introduced to me and they gave me their hunting licenses and identified themselves as members of a varmint hunting club. Probably new members as they did not know much about hunting laws and regulations, or their prior hunting took place in areas not patrolled by game wardens or other law enforcement officers. We made many contacts with members of this "hunting club" whose members were from a large metropolitan area 200 miles from our city.

This particular club would meet on a Friday to start the "hunt" and meet again on Sunday to check-out and determine the winner. Yes, it was a contest and their hunting methods were mostly illegal. At the beginning of the "hunt" they would be told of specific target animals and the method of proof needed to show they had actually killed that animal. I knew that mountain lions were tops as far as points were concerned. Different points were awarded for different species. Proof needed? Maybe it was an ear, a foot, a tail but for sure a small part of the animal that was distinctive to that animal and could be hidden if necessary.

I advised them of the regulations regarding the use of lights at night and their violation and of my intention to cite them both. I went into the camper to check the firearms and to look for evidence of animals that they may have. They might call it "varmint" hunting but some of the animals they pursued had specific seasons when their take by legal methods was allowed.

They had an altered pick-up truck with a camper attached in the bed. This pick-up was altered specifically for this type of hunting with a closable hatch in the camper roof. This alteration was very familiar to me. The passenger or hunter would stand in the camper with the ability to shine the spotlight 360 degrees as the pick-up was slowly driven along the roads. The firearms were also carried on the roof in a secure rack and sand bags were used for shooting support.

Also in the back of the truck was an electronic predator call with a cassette of an injured rabbit that was played in order to bring a target animal into view. They had two rifles, one shotgun, two handguns and two 12 volt spotlights but I found no evidence that they had killed anything. I cited them for "shining a spotlight into the fields and forests from a moving vehicle on a public roadway while possessing a firearm". I seized only the spotlights but if I had found evidence of an animal killed I would have seized one or more of the firearms.

Also the deputy found reason to cite the truck owner for illegal modification of a vehicle and the other for illegal possession of a handgun.

SECURITY AT THE RARE EARTH MINERAL FACILITY

I was asked by my supervisor if I was willing to provide security at a rare earth mining operations facility. This facility produced the majority of the world's demand for light and heavy rare earth minerals in the 1980's that continued into the 1990's and was apparently experiencing some trespass incidents. One way travel from my home to the site for the week's work was just short of 350 miles.

In 1998 operations were suspended and six months prior to my retirement I spent two separate weeks working the night shift from 5:00 p.m. to 5:00 a.m. The director of security at the facility used members from several state law enforcement agencies for this assignment. This job required just one person per shift to be stationed at the facility in a remote desert area. Vehicle patrol was also part of the night's work. Travel to daily sleeping accommodations and meals were to a neighboring state. It was a different patrol situation and thankfully was very quiet during my shifts.

CHAPTER 11

FIELD TRAINING OFFICER ASSIGNMENTS

During the mid 1980's our fish and game department put into operation a "field training officer" program. It was modeled after an existing program developed by a "traditional" police agency in our state. I was part of the team that brought this modern day training program to reality and I was among the initial group of training officers.

The "FTO" program was required of all new hires even if they had prior law enforcement experience. So we had trainees right out of the academy and others with ten plus years of law enforcement experience in their resume. For each trainee, the program began with a week of general orientation usually at the nearest headquarters office to the patrol district where they were assigned. Then they were assigned to three different field training officers for their official training.

Each of these three sessions lasted four weeks at the beginning of our department's program but was later reduced to three weeks per cycle. The last step was a final week with their new supervisor. The three assignments with an FTO were conducted in different areas of the state that usually had different wildlife enforcement issues, terrain, etc. in order to give them a well rounded training experience not to mention working with three different "warden personalities". Daily written evaluations were completed and discussed, then forwarded to their receiving supervisor. Of my fifteen training officer assignments, three were female trainees and my evaluation for one of my male trainees caused me to recommend failure from proceeding to the next step which would have meant being assigned as a solo game warden. My recommendation was upheld.

Something else I did early on with each female trainee that was assigned to me may have gone against protocol or rules but I brought them to my home to meet my wife. In my way of thinking a very logical step as for four weeks the trainee and I would be together every work day and night as required. I think this step was very important for the health of my marriage.

As I was a firearms instructor and range-master I tried to spend some time our first day together at our local gun range to evaluate their proficiency with their issued sidearm and also but very important, to develop a rapport with each of them. The academy had a very good and comprehensive firearms program but this time on the range instilled in me confidence in my "partner" during the next three or four weeks where unknown situations or use of force may be needed.

In this chapter I will describe some incidents that occurred with separate trainees that were handled by each in an exemplary manner. You will note that even though the trainee is asked to make most if not all of the decisions and complete the written reports required some cases take teamwork so the trainer becomes the trainees partner. Toward the end of some of these training assignments I would elect to be out of uniform and stand back so the person(s) contacted would first respond to the authority figure which would be the one of us in uniform.

I continued to be active in this program, in fact I conducted training and evaluations for three separate trainees during my last year of work prior to retirement.

MY FIRST FEMALE TRAINEE

I'm sure you can picture that the purpose of a field training officer program is to prepare officers new to law enforcement as well as current law enforcement officers transferring from other agencies what to expect as they receive "on-the-job" training. You would think that someone pursuing a career in wildlife law enforcement at minimum would have hunting and firearms experience and have a desire to work outdoors in all climates. This was not always the case. I'll outline some of the training subjects that I covered during one of my first training officer assignments in order to describe to you some of the subjects we were required to cover.

This trainee was a well educated young woman with a college degree in biological sciences and who also had experience teaching at a correctional facility. She had no law enforcement background, very little hunting or four-wheel drive vehicle experience. But she had lots of other outdoor related activity in her past. I was her third training officer which meant my four weeks with her would consist of twenty documented "observation" days which had to end with a "yes or no" recommendation by me for her future as a game warden with our department.

Her first training day with me was the day before the opening of our deer season so we were off and running as soon as she arrived. We attended a "pre-opener" meeting with other fish and game staff in the area and contacted and answered questions of members from other local agencies that are authorized to validate the tags of successful hunters. We investigated a report of a dove hunter violation and I familiarized her with the location of the local elk herd.

We then patrolled in the mountains until almost midnight for night hunting deer poachers. A long first day, but our next day while being "only" twelve hours, was busy with hunter contacts in their vehicles, on foot while they hunted and also when in their camps at the end of their hunting day. I wanted her to become familiar with the hunter's equipment, including knives, rifles and other firearms if available and get comfortable with her contacts during checks of licenses, tags and equipment and their deer if they were successful.

She needed to learn to speak like a fellow hunter and become knowledgeable in the habits and appearance of the local wildlife while engaging them in conversation, even when a violation may be suspected. Imagine this, approaching a deer camp at the end of the day, all men, maybe six to eight, rifles leaning everywhere, alcohol, and a campfire going strong while they tell their hunting stories. There may also be a deer or two hanging from a tree nearby or even one hidden from view. For a female game warden recruit this can be a very trying situation. This is how it went.

We were both in uniform and I let her assume the lead during this contact. I remained very close mainly for safety reasons. She overlooked the sexist remarks and jokes and handled the contact with proper conversation and questions while watching their movements in relation to the visible firearms. At the completion of our first camp contact and return to our vehicle I told her that I wanted to go back to the camp for just a minute and would return shortly. I went back and told the hunters what had just occurred during the contact and that I wanted their impression of her professionalism and her future as a game warden. They were impressed and she left them with a feeling of mutual respect. It was a unanimous "yes" vote for her.

We continued our contacts of hunters through the week and she even field dressed a 3X4 buck after a short lesson. We spent time discussing our relationships with other agencies, doing lots of firearms training on and off the range, mountain lion information, trapper training, defensive tactics testing, completed the Water Pollution and the Streambed Alteration training units and some very intense pick-up truck driving in four-wheel drive situations.

You may wonder what became of this "future game warden". After our four weeks together she received a positive overall evaluation from me. She then moved to her initial patrol assignment where her supervisor gave her additional training pertinent to her first assignment. During her service and along with the regular duties she concentrated lots of her time teaching and promoting the hunter education program, and a natural resources volunteer program. She was a state trained "armorer" which meant she conducted periodic inspections of state issued firearms and she also served as a field training officer. She retired after twenty four years of service and now twenty eight years after her initial "training" with me we still keep in touch

148 TROUT OVERLIMIT CAUGHT BY THREE FISHERMEN

Next is an investigation that was primarily handled by a fish and game academy graduate who was assigned to me also during his last training cycle. His training period with me included the opening two weeks of trout season so he was able to make lots of contacts during "out of uniform" and small boat patrols.

Other than our patrol duties dealing with current open seasons and popular activities connected to them we were assigned a training unit dealing with Pollution Investigation. We remained able to respond to and assist with other unplanned activities such as assisting with tranquilizing and placing a radio collar on a mountain lion that was held in a leg hold trap by our wildlife biologist.

He made 543 individual contacts mostly of fishermen that resulted in the issuance of fifteen citations and seven warnings.

Described here is the investigation and outcome of three of the fifteen citations he issued. It was a trout over limit case that involved three men. Just a few trout over limit or a double limit you might think and that is usually the case but what made this case out of the ordinary was the number of trout over limit, the illegal fishing method involved and finally the court imposed sentences.

A small group of concerned fishermen who were true sportsmen made the following observations during their fishing earlier on a Friday in early May and who subsequently made a report to our district office. After receiving the violation report from the office we proceeded to the boat landing or marina office near the boat launch facilities of this very popular lake. My trainee contacted the attendant at the boat rental office who told him, "some fishermen watched three men catch an over limit of trout in one of the back bays of the lake while fishing from rental boat #38". We were given a copy of the rental agreement to boat #38 showing that the boat was first rented three days prior with the last day of rental the next day, Saturday. The employee didn't know where the witnesses were and couldn't tell us how to contact them.

We left the office and were immediately approached by four men who said they were the ones who made the report. Three were in their mid-twenties and one was the father of one of them. They excitedly described their observations saying without a doubt the three men fishing from rental boat #38 had taken an over limit that same day. They described seeing them count fifteen fish on one stringer and more in a basket used for hanging fish in the water while fishing. There were other stringers and they said "they must have fifty to sixty trout they caught that morning". They told us that they were pretty sure the men left the lake area prior to our arrival. Earlier they saw them return to the dock area with their rental boat, unload their equipment and fish then left on foot to the parking area.

They gave us good physical descriptions of the men then described their observations that convinced them that the men had violated the law. One said, "While they were anchored and bait fishing they frequently dumped into the water beside their boat clumps of red or orange stuff that looked like salmon eggs then they would concentrate their lines into that same area". This is referred to as "chumming" where a food attractant is placed into the water to draw fish to the artificially produced feeding station. Putting clumps of salmon eggs called clusters into the water, then using salmon eggs on the hook is a very successful but illegal method of fishing. It was very successful for these men.

After describing what they saw one of the witnesses said, "I video-taped them while they were on their boat, would you like to watch it?" I don't have to say here what our answer was so he rewound the tape to the footage of the fish poachers. While watching the video we confirmed the witnesses' description of the activities onboard the suspect boat and the number of trout caught and in their possession.

The limit was five fish per day per fisherman with a possession limit of ten fish or two daily limits no matter how many days were spent fishing.

We watched as they pulled up a wire basket containing fish and a stringer holding more fish up into their boat. The witnesses said they pulled up their anchor and left the bay returning to the docks. I asked if I could keep the tape for evidence and the "photographer" removed it from the camera and gave it to me. We thanked them for their concern and willingness to see that we got the information. They were glad they had the opportunity to assist us and told us where they were camped if additional information was needed. The video was quite lengthy and described their trip from their home town about 200 miles away. It also showed their fishing activities and it was clear from their discussions among themselves that they were law abiding sportsmen.

While walking toward the rental docks to find #38 we contacted another dock employee and asked him where #38 was located. He showed us and said the renters told the dock employees to stay out of their boat. Kind of strange but the employees had no reason to go into the boat anyway. The reason was clear. There were parts of smashed salmon egg clusters all over the left side and inside bottom of the boat. I took photos of  this evidence and the bow of the boat showing it to be #38. We then checked the area of the cleaning tables and parking lot but did not see the suspects. The rental agreement had only a home address out of town so we didn't know where they may be staying locally. Knowing they had the boat rented the following day, their last, we decided to leave and return early the next morning to attempt contact so we called it a day at 6:00 p.m.

Saturday began for us at 5:30 a.m. Dressed like fishermen and with our fishing gear we drove to the lake and parked in an area away from the designated boat dock parking as we were in my identifiable fish and game patrol pick-up. At 6:15 a.m. we wandered around the parking lot to see if we could spot the three men as there were many other fishermen preparing to go to their boats or going to fish from the nearby shoreline. We went to the slip where #38 was docked the day before. #38 was already gone. We went to where the fish and game boat was docked in the public area of the docks, loaded our gear and joined the rest of the boats leaving for the "fishing grounds" at approximately 7:30 a.m.

Our boat was a twelve foot aluminum boat with no identifiable markings. It fit in with most of the other small fishing boats. We had conducted an undercover patrol of this lake earlier in the week that resulted in four citations and five warnings for small over limits, chumming, and fishing with no license. So my trainee was at home with the plan, to act like fishermen and go to areas to try and locate #38 and watch with binoculars from a distance that would not spook them. We found them at 10:00 a.m. and watched them for about forty five minutes. While they made preparations to leave, their anchor line broke as they tried to pull it off the bottom. They then headed toward the docks with us following at a distance.

They arrived at the docks about 11:30 a.m. with us a short time behind. By 12:30 p.m. they had their fish and equipment stowed in their car, a late model BMW and left the parking area. We returned to our pick-up and again from a distance because we were now in my identifiable pick-up, we followed them to the nearest town about ten miles away.

Once in town they pulled onto a side road and pulled into a parking space at a condominium. We waited to be sure this was their destination. They exited and began unloading fishing equipment from the passenger area and trunk. Having parked around the corner we approached on foot and identified ourselves as fish and game wardens as we were still out of uniform. My trainee took over from this point and asked the appropriate investigative questions.

He asked to see their fishing licenses which they presented to him. He continued asking, "How many trout did you catch this morning?" One of the younger men opened an ice chest containing trout. He again asked, "How many trout did you catch?" The oldest of the three and father of one of the others answered, "Three limits". They transferred these fresh trout from the ice chest to another that was empty. There were seventeen trout total. He asked, "Who caught the two trout that exceeds the limit"? The oldest of the men said, "The fourth fisherman in our group caught them and he should be on his way here now".

During conversation the group said they had been fishing for four days and caught fish every day. My partner asked the oldest where they were keeping their fish and he said they were in the condominium. When he asked to be shown the rest of their fish he said, "The man we are waiting for has the key to the condominium". Knowing the truth about how many were in their fishing party he said, "Look, we've been watching the three of you fishing from rental boat #38 so let's cut the crap". These might be my thoughts and not his exact words but he got the same result. He again asked, "Show us the rest of your fish, please". The oldest of the three then directed us into the condominium where he showed us a shelf full of cleaned and packaged trout. He removed the fish from the refrigerator and placed them into an empty ice chest so we could count them. He was hesitant to open the freezer but when he did we found it to be full of frozen trout. I took the trout outside and counted them in the presence of the older man's son.

He told me that there was no other person with them. "The three of us caught all of the trout". I counted 161 trout from the condominium making a total of 178 trout in their possession.

More discussion produced an admission that they had been chumming to attract the fish to their boat.

All the trout were seized but we returned to each man their maximum possession limit of ten trout to keep. I wonder if

79

they enjoyed eating them and what the mealtime discussion might have been.

We took photos of all the fish and issued each a citation to appear in court for the take and possession of the trout over limit and illegal method of take which was chumming. They were each fined $1,485 for a total of $4,455 plus each were given three years' probation during which time they were not to fish in the state. A pretty worthwhile contact made possible by observant and concerned sportsmen and a trainee dedicated to success.

"ROUTINE" PATROL LEADS TO STOLEN PICK-UP THEN TO METH LAB

For this next training session I was assigned a trainee that just left a more traditional law enforcement agency to join our fish and game department. He had many years experience and left the other agency in good standing like I did about fifteen years prior. Like me he had a love for the outdoors and wildlife and actually lived in a rural area where he was to be assigned after he completed our field training officer program. During our three week session I was assigned to train and evaluate him at the location of his headquarters assignment. So during our second week together I packed up and teamed with him to patrol on his turf so to speak. The last day of this week together was a Tuesday so we didn't think too much would happen that wouldn't be "routine" but we went out looking anyway. I thought that if nothing else we could discuss the past week and his knowledge acquired so far during our patrols together.

It was upland game season and the area we chose for this last day was a fairly popular but secluded location for quail hunters. We were in a marked, identifiable patrol vehicle and in uniform for this patrol. We left the paved road about 6:00 a.m. and patrolled into an area of the county that had many side roads and motorcycle trails sometimes opening up to unimproved camping areas that have obviously been used for many years due to the number of fire rings and trash scattered about the area. Lots of secluded canyons branched off to great hideaways if privacy was preferred.

At 7:30 a.m. as we drove up from the bottom of one of the canyons we saw a reflection from a pick-up with a camper shell parked on a hillside high and to our right. It looked like it was stuck on a narrow motorcycle trail and about to roll over. It was heading down hill and its' doors were open. We parked and hiked up to the pick-up. We saw no one and as we got to the pick-up we saw that the in-dash radio and door speakers had been hastily removed evidenced by the wires hanging under the dash and from the side panels on each open door. Contents of the truck glove box were scattered around the interior.

From this location we could now see a motor-home parked further up the canyon about eighty yards away in a level zone as if set up for camping. We had no outside radio contact with other agencies where we were so we opted to split up so notification of our find of a suspected stolen pick-up could be made.

I remained in the area and continued to observe the area while he drove to the top of the canyon to advise the local sheriff's office of our suspicion giving them the license number of the pick-up. It returned as reported stolen from a city about one-hundred miles away. Due to the remoteness of our location and being a good mile and a half from a blacktop road he advised the responding agency that he would meet them at the blacktop and side road junction and guide them to the scene.

He then re-contacted me with the information and left me to maintain security and observations of the area including, of course, the parked motor-home. While I watched for the next hour and a half I observed a woman appearing to be in her early twenties and in pajamas leave the motor-home for a short time to the nearby bushes then return back inside.

Upon the return of my partner he advised me that he had to guide an aircraft in to identify the site location for a ground unit to respond when one could free up from other activities but at least an hour later. I told him about the woman's exit and reentry. We then decided to contact the occupants of the motor-home to see if she-or they-had any knowledge of the stolen pick-up.

We drove to the motor-home and parked in a defensive position a short distance away. We were in uniform and would be immediately recognized as law enforcement officers. All of the windows were covered with curtains that blocked our view to the inside. The loud generator of the motor-home was running and when we approached we saw an over and under rifle shotgun combination lying on a plastic bucket next to the side door of the motor-home. Believing our presence was not known, I checked the firearm, found it was loaded and for safeties sake I unloaded it.

We positioned on each side of the door and my partner pounded hard on the door while yelling "hello" several times. The generator was still very loud. After several attempts the woman I had seen previously opened the door and looked out. He asked her about any knowledge of the pick-up and she answered, "It was there when I arrived last night". Then a young man, also in his early twenties pushed his way into the doorway looking at my partner but not saying anything. He exhibited a very protective attitude that increased our caution. My partner asked, "Are there any others inside the motor-home"? They both immediately replied "no, just our dog". She said their dog was a Doberman but was friendly and called him to the door. He asked if they would mind coming out of the motor-home and they answered "no" and stepped out while opening the door wider as they did.

This wider opening of the door allowed me to see an additional man inside. I stepped to the doorway and seeing empty hands I yelled for him to slowly step out and to the ground with the others. He was also young and was probably sleeping when we arrived. He complied and now all three were asked if there were any others inside and again the answer was "no".

As my partner watched the three subjects I cautiously entered and saw a rifle on the floor where the third subject had been standing near a couch made up as a bed. The magazine was loaded but there was no round in the chamber. Looking back, this could have been a life saving consideration being some serious crimes were about to be discovered and they probably knew it. I continued my search for additional subjects while in the midst of a strong chemical odor.

I cleared the motor-home finding no additional subjects but while checking the far back section found a full scale, up and running narcotics lab. I exited and advised my partner of my find. He entered and confirmed my find. Only one choice available here, handcuff, search and control all three while being thankful about their only true statement to us, "the dog is friendly". Ever wonder why officers have more than one set of cuffs available on their belts?

I kept control at the scene while telling them how nervous it can become for one officer to be in control of three subjects. "Nervous people can react quickly in a situation like this". My partner again located a spot that allowed radio contact with the local agency and returned advising me of their pending response.

With our location marked by the previous fly over by law enforcement aircraft it didn't take but a half an hour to see our first response from a senior deputy sheriff. Of course he confirmed our suspicions and took the three into his custody. He called for their Narcotics Enforcement Team and a short time later seven more officers arrived at the scene and an animal control officer was still en-route.

The stolen pick-up was easily linked to the same suspects as it was stolen from their city of residence and there were items visible at the motor-home that obviously came from the same pick-up. Not a coincidence. Also during the search by the deputies a loaded revolver was found under the pillow on the couch where the third suspect was first seen. My partner and I were now done and released from the scene at 11:00 a.m.

A subsequent report by the Narcotic Enforcement Team described this lab as being equipped to produce two pounds of methamphetamine every twenty four hour period. At that time the street value was approximately eighteen-thousand dollars per pound. They also told us this lab was the largest "mobile" narcotics lab they had seen in their county to date.

Lots of travel time was spent, mainly by me as I lived a ways away, to attend the court proceedings that carried on because of defendants "failure to appear" and skipping out on "bail". Each defendant was assigned their own "public defender" and that caused further scheduling conflicts and what I would consider "snafus". We never had to appear for final dispositions on any of them as the charges were all probably settled with "pleas", reduced sentences or they were never seen again. However; the evidence and the legality of the arrests would stand up in any court proceeding.

TRAINING ABOUT BEARS
Not an enforcement situation but part of a training day that I dedicated for the purpose of teaching another trainee about bears. It was mid-summer and we finished checking fishermen at a couple of high country lakes and patrolled downstream into an area with several campgrounds. The river that ran through this high valley was very popular with fly fishermen and family camping. Hiking trails, a pack station and some geologic wonders attracted vacationers with all kinds of interests. Then there were the bears.

The first lesson to be learned was that bears are creatures of habit and return to sources of past food availability. The common term back then is that the "bears become habituated to humans", and to the human habits that can benefit them. I chose this area for bear training because there was an ongoing rash of bear intrusions into the campgrounds and entries into tents and break-ins to vehicles in this area.

We parked just beyond the campground boundary where there were few people then walked the camps receiving stories from campers regarding their bear experiences. We saw damaged ice chests and some that weren't damaged but had none the less been opened with the contents eaten and, or scattered around. He was able to see tracks of different size bears and learned about their most popular attractants. I was hoping that we would see one or more bears but being mid-day they were absent. We decided to walk back toward our vehicle through the surrounding forest area where we might be able to find a bear or two spending some time away from people or maybe just hiding out.

We had a nice walk back and as we got closer to our pick-up we heard a rattling noise coming from that direction. First thought was, "is somebody breaking into the pick-up to steal equipment?" When we separated and snuck in close enough we saw one of the bears that we were searching for, in the bed of our truck and working on the lid of our ice chest that contained our lunch and drinks. I wouldn't be surprised if the bear watched as we parked and left on our walk. We made a slow approach making sure he saw us and we got closer only when he decided to get down and leave. Thankfully, our lunch was still okay.

CHAPTER 12

LICENSE AND TAG VIOLATIONS

Fish and game and wildlife agencies have many different license and tag requirements for sport and commercial activities required for the take of many different species. I'll outline here sport licensing of which there are many different types beyond just fishing and hunting. There are separate tags for deer, elk, bear, moose, etc. and they all have their regulations regarding their possession and use.

The most popular location by the sportsmen for the purchase of sport licenses in our state was sporting goods stores, large and small, marinas, resorts, and other businesses that cater to fishermen and hunters in one way or another. Now in my later years of retirement I know that the internet is now involved big time in licensing of both resident and nonresident licenses and tags. I dealt with some of these private license agents on a regular basis regarding violations of persons they sold a license to as well as for illegal actions conducted by their agency, some accidental and probably due to untrained seasonal or part-time help but some intentional.

ILLEGAL ACTIONS BY A LICENSE AGENT

The long-time owner of one of our popular sporting goods store who was also a license agent did what I thought was a stupid thing one year that was detected by someone he occasionally hunted deer with. This person obviously did not agree with what this license agent "friend" of his did so he contacted me and "put the ball in my court" so to speak. This informant was pretty sure the agent possessed two hunting licenses which more importantly allowed him to purchase two deer tags. He may have done this every year to give himself an added "bonus" related to his hunting activities, I don't know, but we stopped him this particular year and the following year.

I worked with our department licensing office to obtain records from the agency he owned. While viewing the records submitted by his agency to our department which showed the dates hunting licenses were sold, their numbers, and the name of the licensee, it didn't take long to see links between the names and addresses listed for two of the licenses just six numbers apart and from his agency. On one application he used his nickname and his business address. The second application had his true name and his home address. He followed up by purchasing a deer tag to go with each license as only one deer tag per hunter was allowed.

If I wanted two hunting licenses would I buy them from the same agency; and especially from my own agency? I think not. When I had the paperwork together I contacted him and requested to see his licenses and tags. As an agent he knew, or should have known, that information on his agency license and tag sales was available to wardens. He produced both of them and handed them over. I seized both of his hunting licenses and deer tags and cited him to appear in court.

He came to court with counsel and was found guilty after a court trial. He was fined $255 and you might think a light sentence but two months later he received a notice from our department removing his store from the privilege of being a license agency. That administrative action punished him more than any fine could have. But also know that he had no deer tags for hunting that year and was not allowed tags the following year.

REVOCATION OF A GUIDE LICENSE

Another popular commercial activity was to become a guide, licensed with our department. Guide means any person who is engaged in the business of packing or guiding, or who for compensation assists another person in hunting or fishing or to locate, take, photograph, or view any bird, mammal, fish, reptile or amphibian and includes any person who transports other persons or their equipment or both to hunting or fishing areas. Sportsmen using a guide must still have in possession the required licenses and tags and they have to abide by all laws and regulations including shooting or catching themselves whatever species they are pursuing.

We had several licensed guides that lived and worked in our community and some of the neighboring towns as well. Their clients were mostly from out of our area and not familiar with our wildlife habitat and locations where they may be successful in their hunting or fishing trips. In some cases they may be new to the "sport" and want to learn how it is done. As I stated previously the clients of a licensed guide must obey all laws and regulations but I will add here that a person with a guides' license should also set an example by obeying all wildlife related laws and regulations themselves. A guide's license may be revoked if he is convicted of a law or regulation pursuant to the take or possession of wildlife. You probably figured out where I'm going with this by now.

I got to know a local man because of his "attitude" about obeying fish and game laws and specifically because of three separate violations and convictions. But more importantly after these convictions of fish and game laws he was still issued a guide's license by our department. After some research I found out that applicants were not being investigated to determine if they had a record of any violations prior to issuance of a guide license. Here is what I explained through channels to our licensing department.

On March 1 of this particular year a guide license was issued to this local resident who had a history of disregard for fish and game laws and regulations. I was involved in three separate convictions for violations he committed during the deer seasons four and five years prior. His hunting privileges were revoked by the court for a period of three years and also a short time later by our fish and game commission also for three years.

So now with his revocation period over, he applied for and was issued a license to guide hunters. You can imagine how I felt when I found out that sportsmen were paying big bucks to this "poacher" to most likely learn how to circumvent the law. I found this out, not from our department but by others who knew him and his illegal sport hunting ethic and history.

These were not simple mistakes or administrative errors but flagrant, intentional violations I'll describe to you. Law enforcement officers and recreation personnel of the forest service assisted with two of the cases. I had a wonderful and very helpful relationship with personnel from the forest service. We were always ready to assist each other and sometimes I patrolled with some of their officers. I assisted them with some of their training such as PR-24 baton certification and firearms training and qualification. I also conducted pre-season meetings for officers of other agencies to advise them about fish and game laws and regulations and found the meetings to be well worth the time spent.

This is done for a couple of reasons, the first being that most of the officers from other agencies are very willing and able because of their duties to provide assistance to us but as officers they are also authorized to validate the tags of deer that are presented to them. Hunters are required to have their tag validated by the nearest authorized person on the route being followed from where the deer was taken and prior to arriving at its' destination. This meant that an un-validated tag on a deer at the home of a hunter would have been illegal.

The first violation occurred on Friday night prior to the Saturday morning opening of deer season. The "future guide" was observed by forest service personnel as he drove his pick-up onto forest property through a manned information center. He had one passenger and two uncased rifles on the rear window gun rack. According to the forest service attendant they were uncooperative and would not give the required information such as the reason for the entry and their intended destination.

They left the center but when only one-hundred feet away and moving slowly. they began shining a spotlight from the left side, to the front and then to the right side. The light was shined at ground level and in a zone where deer may be located. This was about 9:30 p.m. This pick-up was stopped by a forest ranger two hours later several miles up the road still shining the spotlight while driving on the forest roads.

During this contact the suspect who was also the driver, was described as being uncooperative, disrespectful, and evasive. Even after warning them of the violation they did not comply. Friday night before the deer opener was pretty busy so I was unable to respond to assist. They were able to get the necessary information on the driver, the vehicle and their activities so I was able to file a complaint on information and belief with our local court. The violation was the act of shining a spotlight on any highway or in any field, woodland or forest where game mammals, fur-bearing mammals or non-game mammals are commonly found while having in possession or under control any firearm or weapon with which such mammal could be killed.

That was the night before the deer opener. Now let's go to the Monday after opening weekend, just three days later, which is often a day for wardens to get caught up with report writing, filing cases in court and checking with the meat markets to get a feel for the success of the opener. That's what I was doing but many thanks for another great assist from the forest service.

One of the forest rangers who witnessed the Friday night spotlighting was patrolling in the same general area mid-day the following Monday. I knew him well and he was a very conscientious man and serious about his job as a forest ranger as all of them that I knew were. During my continuing law enforcement relationship with them it was obvious that they were keeping current with their training and they presented themselves very professionally at all times.

Now it's Monday and almost 1:00 p.m. when this same officer recognized the man who he warned about spotlighting the previous Friday night. He was walking up a canyon, hitchhiking. Without hesitation he picked him up mainly to find out what he was doing. His vehicle, the same one he was driving Friday night was parked at the top of the canyon.

During the short ride he told he ranger that he was hunting with some "buddies" and one of them had shot a buck lower down in the canyon and that he needed to get to his pick-up to get a saw in order to help him cut up the buck so it could be carried out to the road. The ranger left him at his truck and left as if he was leaving the area. He got to an area where he could watch his actions with binoculars. His actions became suspicious as he drove back down the road. The hunter seemed hesitant about each subsequent move. After quite a while he took a saw and a day pack and left on foot into the brushy area near where he was first seen hitchhiking.

After quite a while he returned to his vehicle with the rear hind quarters of a deer. After a cigarette and a rest he again left and headed into the brush. He returned with the front shoulders including the head and antlers. The ranger saw that there was no tag attached to the antlers as required. The ranger moved further up the road and parked at the main intersection at the top. He waited at that location very visible in order to see which direction he would go and to see if he would stop to have the buck validated. But "He smiled and waved as he drove by me", as reported by the ranger.

The ranger got word to me through channels. I picked up a neighboring warden and we proceeded to the road where we thought he would be exiting the mountains. It was now getting dark, after 5:00 p.m., and we continued up the road thinking we were sure to meet him as we travelled the same road. We saw his pick-up approaching, allowed him to pass, turned around then pulled him over. He was alone and of course we knew he had a buck in his camper. As our investigation continued, we found along with the untagged 4X3 point buck, he had his wife's unused deer tag, and he had his deer tag that was not punched but had two dates written on it indicating the opening day as well as this day as days he took a deer. I cited him for possession of an untagged deer, failure to punch and attach his tag to his deer, possession of a tag belonging to another, and altering a tag.

Five months later, he and his attorney appeared in court to answer the charges on the violations that occurred over the four day period during the prior deer opener. He was found guilty and fined $335 and placed on two years probation. He was cited for another violation the following year when he was on probation. He bought a deer tag when he was not to hunt during his probationary period. Therefore, his probationary period was extended another year. That brought his history up to date. So when this information was forwarded to our licensing branch they immediately revoked his license to guide and requested he surrender it to our department.

ALTER LICENSE DATE

This contact started out with a citation issued to a forty-eight year old man for fishing in a local creek without a fishing license in possession. He told me he bought one about five months prior but "left it at camp somewhere on the road back to town". Instead of playing "his" game I played mine and cited him for fishing with no fishing license in possession. I told him all he had to do was mail it to the court and the fine would be reduced.

The court received a fishing license from him the next week with his reduced fine of fifty dollars. It was dated ten days prior to the date of the citation. What happened to the "five months prior"? Two days later I picked up the license from the court and contacted the local agent that sold the license. Their records showed no fishing licenses were sold by them on that day. I was lucky enough to have contacted the same employee that was working on the day of the citation. I described him to her and she stated without hesitation that a man came to the store the same date as the citation and purchased a fishing license and told her that, "I was cited earlier for not having one". The issue date on the license was altered by changing one of the numbers.

I gave the court the information from my investigation and they issued a warrant for his arrest for $500. It took eleven months but he was arrested at his home about 200 miles from where he was cited and paid the fine. Just a little more work but our efficient licensing system and knowledgeable court made it fairly easy for me to play "his" game.

UNSUCCESSFUL STAKEOUT FOR HUNTER OF ILLEGAL DEER

This deer season investigation was probably a tag violation and or license violation. Either the shooter of the deer had no tag or he had already used it, anyway about 9:00 a.m. on the Sunday of opening weekend a hunter found an untagged field dressed buck partially hidden in some brush and not far from town. He showed me the location and I told him to leave the area in case the illegal shooter returned.

My plan was to remove my pick-up from the area and return on foot to watch for someone to return to the deer. I used the rest of my Sunday watching and stayed until well after dark. I was glad I had enough to eat and drink in my day pack.

About 9 p.m. I went to the location and the deer was still there. Being it was properly dressed I decided to pick it up and take it to a local agency that butchered and used the meat for needy people. I was pretty certain that the shooter saw the reporting hunter or me and stayed away for fear of being caught. It turned out to be an unsuccessful but restful day for me.

CHAPTER 13

FISHING VIOLATIONS

In most of the areas I worked, freshwater fishing was very popular. When describing freshwater fishing one has to distinguish between cold and warm water species. Salmon, steelhead and trout would most likely be found in cold water habitats whereas bass, catfish, walleye, pike and sunfish would be found in warm water habitats.

Most of my fish and game time was spent in locations where both habitats were available for catching many different species of fish. Naturally the high elevation lakes and streams would be home to the cold water species that seemed to be the most popular for anglers. Areas where there was more activity would be where I would necessarily spend more of my patrol time and effort although seasons and weather also had to be reckoned with and planned for.

In warmer climates night fishing was popular and in the high mountains during early spring ice fishing was pretty popular. Firearms were legal to be carried by fisherman and some did; however, they all had knives available for cleaning their catch so an awareness of this fact was necessary plus knives and other weapons were always on hand by campers'.

TROUT PLANTING FROM HATCHERIES

A great time for me to monitor people fishing for trout was when our local fish hatchery was making its' plants into our lakes and streams. In fact during the summer people would wait for the department truck to appear and follow it to the lake or stream where they released the fish. They were catchable size and there was no regulation about giving them time to spread out before fishing for them.

This was a good time for me to hide my patrol vehicle and make a quick change to look like a fisherman. I used a multi-pocketed fishing vest and would get in position to observe several fishermen at the same time. While "fishing" myself with no hook on my lure, I would keep track of their take by putting pebbles in a pocket designated for a specific person. I could keep track of four people this way without any confusion on my part. Some days were very productive for me and other days had mostly legal fishermen, but that was a good thing.

FIVE FISHERMEN DRINKING BEER – NO LICENSES

"Okay, when did you buy them?" I asked after five fishermen told me they bought them but left them in the parking lot. Four of them gave me dates that would be valid for the current season and one said he had one last year but forgot to renew it. He was the one honest guy in the group. They didn't want to return to the parking area, about a half mile away. One said, "man we ain't drank all our beers yet and it's a long way back." They were all well over twenty one and drinking beer mid-morning was not a problem except for the amount. But as they thought a little more a couple of them told me they weren't even fishing.

They didn't know but by using my binoculars from my "favorite pre-contact vantage point" across the lake I knew the real story before making contact with them. When I told them that I needed to see the licenses of those who left them in their vehicle, their friendly attitude changed and as they began picking up their equipment and empty beer cans they uttered some unfriendly words to me. As they ramped up their attitude so did I.

I was very truthful with them, first by saying that I was uncomfortable being outnumbered five to one. I told them how I wanted the walk back to the parking area to work. "Single file with space in between and no talking and I will be taking up the rear." I must have gotten my point across because they were cooperative all during the way back and even during the next forty-five minutes while I issued five citations. I like to think that when they return home if they weren't too ashamed to admit they were pinched by a fish and game guy the word might get out to a few friends and just maybe a few more licenses would be bought. They paid their fines probably because they didn't want anything crazy showing up on their records.

FRESH CAUGHT TROUT FOR SALE

The apprehension of violators selling sport caught fish was not common in the areas I worked. Trout and bass were the common species found in the lakes and streams in the areas of the state where I had been assigned during most of my career. Sport fishing laws did not allow for the selling of any fish taken with a sport-fishing license.

In this case the defendant had good intentions but was none the less violating a fish and game law. Our office received a report of a notice posted on the bulletin board in a mini-mart not far from town. It read "22 cleaned and frozen trout, 10-14 inches long, ready to cook, $20, will deliver" and included a local phone number. I called the number which was answered by a woman and stated that I saw the advertisement and that I was interested in buying two limits and arranged to meet her at a location close to the mini-mart.

I changed out of uniform and used my own truck to go to the "meet". I waited about ten minutes for her to show up. Upon her arrival she got out of her car with the frozen trout in a plastic bag.

I asked to see them and she handed me the bag. I opened it and saw several small rainbow trout that appeared to be from local fish hatchery plants. We finalized the price, made the deal. I then identified myself and advised her of the violation. She said she was not aware of breaking any laws. She said her son caught them and the money was to be for his college education.

I issued her a citation, kept the fish as evidence and advised her to remove any notices that may remain posted. I'm sure some "mean warden" stories spread around her neighborhood.

TOO MANY LINES AND ILLEGAL BAIT

There was a very popular reservoir ten miles north of town that was planted with small trout but also contained some very large brown trout in excess of twenty pounds. Because fishing was allowed at night, the cover of darkness made the illegal activities harder to identify. Violations such as multiple lines in the water and the use of illegal bait i.e., live fish to take the large brown trout were frequent and by the same small group of "sportsmen".

At the beginning of my fish and game career only one line was allowed per fisherman then in the later years two lines were allowed. This regulation change didn't matter to some as they would use three, four or five lines when they thought they could get away with it. They had a favorite area along the rocky shoreline of this reservoir that was a tough climb down the steep bank where they would spend most of the night fishing.

My enforcement contacts in this area began by checking for and identifying vehicles parked in a little used and concealed place that was out of site from any of the roads in the area. If vehicles were found then I made a fairly long drive to the opposite side of the reservoir where fishing activity could be monitored with binoculars or my spotting scope. When violations were observed and documented, I would make a trip back to the other side of the reservoir and hiked down the bank to make contact. The first time I made contact with fishermen here I got burned.

Without prior knowledge of violations and hoping to see how many lines they were using and the bait they were using I had to check for violations upon my arrival down the steep bank. Well, with them always having a lit cigarette in their hand it was very easy to burn each line that was in the water. This made it pretty tough to prove violations; therefore, the prior distant observations became necessary. Sometimes two of us would team up, one to observe and the other to make the contacts. It wasn't easy but it worked pretty well and we issued several citations using this method.

STOLEN VEHICLE IN POSSESSION OF FOUR FISHERMEN

A gated and locked reservoir in a canyon ten miles from town that I described in the previous account was a popular spot for year round fishing. No vehicle access except authorized vehicles so fishermen had to walk about two hundred yards to the water then could walk the couple of miles to the upper end fishing anywhere in between. Large brown trout and smaller but nice sized rainbows were available. I worked it different ways. By checking out both the lower and upper parking lots I would get a feel for activity because a parked vehicle meant fishermen. Also the activity could be checked by vehicle access high on either side of the canyon walls as I described previously.

This day I opted to walk in from the lower parking lot even though there weren't a lot of vehicles parked there. I would check for fishing success and to see if all had their fishing licenses in possession. Sound like a "routine" morning? I parked my patrol vehicle in the parking lot with the rest of the vehicles, maybe three or four were there. When I got to the water, what few people there was were scattered along the shoreline and were concentrating on their fishing. Because of a relatively short walk most people, especially if they had been there before, would carry in an ice chest to bring in beer and hopefully use it to take out trout and the empty beer cans and bottles.

As I observed the fishermen I dialed in to a group of four young adult males. I watched them long enough to confirm that they each were fishing. They were having fun and doing lots of drinking. Sometimes I would concentrate on groups like this observing them for litter violations but I had a feeling these guys may not be "license compliant". I climbed down the short but steep bank and greeted them. They were friendly and had some questions about the reservoir and the fish species it contained.

We chatted a little until I asked to see their fishing licenses. It got pretty quiet but one of them who had most likely been there before said they were in their car that was back in the parking lot. The others didn't say anything but just agreed with the "spokesman". Plus they had no form of identification with them so I really didn't know who I was talking to.

I explained to them that I needed to see their licenses so told them I would accompany them back to their car for a quick check. They picked up their poles, equipment and what beer they had left and we walked back to the gate and into the parking lot.

Our vehicles were parked front to front and they opened the doors and trunk and put their stuff away. They knew I was waiting to see their licenses and other identification but they were just talking quietly among themselves. In the mean time I advised the sheriff's office of my location and gave them the license number of the car. The dispatcher advised me that the car was reported stolen from a city about 250 miles away. This happened pretty fast. I didn't know if they heard the radio but things didn't feel right about them. I immediately released my shotgun from its' electric mount and exited my vehicle with it in hand and pointed at them from behind the door. I slowly and clearly gave them these instructions, "Step away from the car, separate from each other, hands out of pockets and visible and do only as I direct". I did not approach them but kept them at this distance and under observation. I gave further information to the sheriff's dispatcher and she said the highway patrol was en-route. It only took them a couple of minutes.

With four to take into custody they sent two units. We had a good working relationship and they knew game wardens worked solo.

When the four were arrested and under control and with their identification in hand I confronted them about their fishing licenses. None of them had one and admitted that they had not purchased one either so it only took a few minutes for me to issue four citations thanks to the patience of the arresting officers. After all, I had to get something out of this as well.

CHAPTER 14

CLOSED SEASON DEER VIOLATIONS

Our mule deer population was largely migratory. They spent late spring to fall in the high country and would travel over high mountain passes to areas of more moderate climate with plenty of food. The reverse would take place from late fall and through the winter months. They would spend this time on our side of the mountains. Many of them would be available to hunters during early fall hunting season and during the winter the local schools would have field trips to the winter ranges. My children experienced this opportunity to observe several hundred deer in their habitat. I was asked on occasion by teachers to accompany the trips.

Not all people respected the laws against taking the wintering deer after the season for hunting them was over. Here are a few incidents describing the actions of a few who disregard these laws.

"WE ARE JUST RABBIT HUNTING"

A couple of days before Christmas on a clear but cold and windy Saturday afternoon, it was just perfect for watching my favorite football team play. I just put more wood in our wood stove when I got a phone call from a concerned citizen. He reported hearing some gunshots in some foothills about fifteen miles out of town. I had already answered and took care of a call from a citizen earlier who reported a sick or injured golden eagle on the ground just outside of town. I went to the area, found it, and then picked up some material for temporary housing at my home. So instead of just relaxing the remainder of the day I answered another phone call, this one about hearing gunshots.

This person said he saw no one and didn't know the reason for the shots but wanted me to know in case it involved illegal activity. There were many legal and logical reasons for gun fire in this area. Quail, chukar and rabbit seasons were open and all three species occurred in the reported area. Also it was not unusual to have target shooters in the area especially during vacation time for kids. But deer season was not open and the area was prime habitat for wintering deer and was known as "winter deer range" where sportsmen, families, and even school field trips took advantage of the great opportunity to see lots of deer in their natural habitat.

The bucks were in rut and had not lost their antlers yet so deer hunters would often be seen checking out the large racks they were unable to find during the hunting season. This was a good thing for game wardens because honest hunters and sportsmen, and that describes all but a very few, had a possessive and caring attitude toward the deer herds. Also our management programs monitored the overall health of the herds and made determinations regarding the time and length of the open seasons.

This again was good for wardens as most of them would not hesitate to report violations or suspicious activity. Actually violation reports from sportsmen were much more common than reports from non-hunting citizens. It is understandable that a non- hunting citizen may not know about seasons or hunting methods and therefore would not feel confident about making an official report. They also may not know the appropriate person or agency to contact to report a wildlife related crime or something that was suspicious to them.

I guarantee that sportsmen in the community I lived knew where I lived and how to contact me. In most of my years as a game warden my telephone number was listed in the phone book. Our agency required it but also paid for it minus our personal calls of course. We also had our patrol vehicles at home making for timely responses if needed. Did I have trouble making the decision to get into uniform go and see what I could find about the reported gunshots? Or did I think to myself they were "probably legal hunters or target shooters"? This was an easy decision for me. I was at the general area of the reported gunshots in fifteen minutes.

It was now 4:15 p.m. and the sun was behind the snow covered mountains to the west and the wind was blowing pretty strong but variable. I drove along an unimproved dirt road to a location where I could observe the area being careful to remain out of view. I used my variable power, 20X by 45X power spotting scope to survey the area while listening for additional gun fire.

Approximately fifteen minutes later I spotted a pick-up truck with a camper shell that was parked well beyond my location and just off the same dirt road along a fence line.

Another fifteen minutes of observation revealed no one in the area and the pick-up appeared to be unoccupied and I heard no shots fired. As the terrain was not flat but had mild hills and gullies filled with large boulders I was able to slowly drive the dirt road to the parked pick-up watching as I went and hoping that I was not observed. This took just about thirty minutes.

When I got to the pick-up I made a quick visual inspection of the interior only noting that there was a large brown tarp on the bed of the pick-up inside the camper shell. The rear window of the camper was open. I checked the ground for tracks hoping to determine how many exited the pick-up and whether there were any dogs. I saw adult size foot prints indicating that several occupants left the truck. I saw no dog tracks, which makes "sneaking" on people lots easier and I was able to determine the direction of travel of the occupants that showed they all went the same direction.

Sundown was approaching by this time and the cold wind was increasing. I retrieved my 7X35 power binoculars from my pick-up and began scanning the surrounding area concentrating on their suspected direction of travel and possibly their general location. I used the aspects of the terrain and low vegetation as concealment and moved approximately fifty yards to a better vantage point. It was here that I got my first view of three adult males walking in a single file and heading toward the road I had driven up a while ago.

The person in the lead was carrying a small deer across his shoulders and behind his neck while holding the legs down and across his front. The other two each had a rifle. As the suspects continued toward the road I lost sight of them so I decided to seek a different vantage point. When I got into a different position I saw them, now behind some bushes and rocks about one-hundred and fifty yards away but now looking up the hill toward me. I should add here that the distances referred to are from my actual paces conducted the next day. Obviously I had been discovered as now they began retreating faster, using concealment from bushes and rocks as they tried to evade me. I turned and went directly to my pick-up where I contacted the sheriff's office, gave them a brief description of the violation and the pick-up description and license number. I also asked for their assistance as the closest available game warden was seventy miles away.

I then drove back down the road in the direction of the fleeing men. As I approached the point in the road where they were headed I saw one of them trying to hide in some bushes along the road. As I continued my approach by vehicle I used my public address system to order him out onto the road in the open where I could see him. He responded immediately. I then exited my vehicle and advised him to keep his hands open and where I could see them and to remain in place.

It was obvious that this man was the one I saw carrying the deer as his hooded sweatshirt was stained red in the neck, shoulder and arm areas. He also had red stains on his hands, jeans and boots. Also obvious was what appeared to be deer hair along with the suspected deer blood. I conducted a cursory field search and requested identification. He possessed a valid driver's license that showed him to be twenty-nine years of age and that showed he lived in a town about twenty miles away.

An hour had now passed since I first arrived in this area. It was now 5:15 p.m. I placed this first suspect under arrest and took him into custody for taking deer during the closed season. His first statement to me was that he had been hunting rabbits alone and left them in the bushes back behind where he came out of the brush. He said he was heading back up the road to get his truck which was the pick-up with the camper I had checked earlier.

Of course I knew this to be untrue and after searching him, I handcuffed him and placed him in my patrol vehicle. I advised the sheriff's office of one in custody and asked for one of their units to meet me for transport of my prisoner as additional suspects and evidence were not accounted for and I felt I shouldn't leave the area. I also asked the game warden that was seventy miles away to meet me to assist with the investigation that might possibly continue for several more hours. I was unable to get a timely response by a sheriff's deputy that I found out later was due to radio transmission problems with his dispatch. That caused me to continue my investigation on scene with my arrestee under my control.

With the suspect in my patrol vehicle we continued to travel toward the area where I suspected the others to be hiding. It was now completely dark and continued windy. I couldn't see much and due to the wind was unable to hear much either. I had no luck locating the other armed suspects. I decided to continue my search for the other suspects and evidence on foot by locating the spot where I last saw the suspects before they disappeared from my view.

While keeping the "in custody" poacher in close control we continued a search of the area. I kept him in close control and continually asked him if he was all right or if he was experiencing any great difficulty. His only reply was that he was tired from walking a long distance earlier in the day. Having no luck we returned to my patrol vehicle then drove to a location where I finally was able to meet with a sheriff's deputy who took control of my arrestee. I seized from the suspect his green hooded sweatshirt that had the blood and hair on it as I didn't want to lose this piece of evidence. He also requested that I secure his pick-up as he left the keys on the floor. He wanted the keys returned to him. This custodial transfer took place at approximately 6:30 p.m.

I met the responding game warden at approximately 7:00 p.m. on a county road a short distance from the scene. I secured my pick-up got in with him and we drove up the road toward the pick-up truck the suspect said belonged to him in order to secure it per his request. This gave me a chance to fill my partner in on the details of the past three hours.

While we proceeded slowly with lights out toward the area, headlights from a vehicle were seen coming toward us on the same road. We continued and met the vehicle which was the same pick-up claimed by the arrested suspect as belonging to him. The red light was activated and shined on the pick-up to be sure they knew that we were law enforcement. When we stopped my partner and I got out and with cover from my partner I approached remaining outside the headlight beam.

I saw three people in the cab of the pick-up. Two were adult males and the third was a juvenile male. I requested the two adults to slowly exit while keeping their empty hands visible and over their heads. Seeing the approximate age and size of the juvenile I allowed him to remain in the pick-up.

As soon as the adults had exited I was asked about my authority to make such requests of them. I was in uniform, in a marked fish and game patrol vehicle plus they knew the reason for my presence so I saved that discussion until I felt somewhat secure during this contact. I conducted a cursory field search of each one and asked each one for identification while making "small talk".

The driver was twenty-seven and his brother, the right side passenger was twenty-six. I was told that the pick-up belonged to their brother. The juvenile was seven and the son of the suspect I had just taken into custody. He was shivering and had tears running down his cheeks. His pants were torn at both knees but he otherwise appeared uninjured. I asked him to remain in the pick-up and try and get warm. Had this same scenario occurred a few years later I may have been compelled to engage child protective services to ensure this child's welfare but the role of child welfare and of child protection was just now being expanded and understood.

Two rifles were visible in a gun rack located across the rear window and when asked about other firearms I was advised of another rifle located behind the seat. While removing each rifle I asked who the owner was for identification purposes. We seized the three rifles as evidence: a Winchester Model 94 lever action, 25-35 caliber; a Winchester Model 67, .22 caliber; and a Revelation Model 150M, .22 caliber and determined ownership of each. I was told that the Winchester Model 94 belonged to the passenger, the Revelation Model 150M belonged to the driver and the Winchester Model 67 belonged to their brother who was in custody. This was important for the prosecution during trial. Also seized from the pick-up were 2 boxes of ammunition from the cab and a wood saw with fresh blood, hair and bits of meat lodged in its' teeth from the bed of the pick-up. There was no deer or deer parts in the pick-up.

I advised the subjects of my observations and of the investigation and looked at their clothing and exposed skin for blood and hair. They did not wish to answer any other questions regarding their activities. I told them of the wishes of their brother regarding the security of his pick-up and they answered that they would return it to their brother's house as they were visiting him. We then accompanied them from the area to the county road where my pick-up was parked and watched as they left the area.

We went back to the area of the arrest in order to locate the additional evidence that was obviously still out there. We followed the suspected route they took when they were first spotted by me earlier in the afternoon. It was completely dark with no moon and a very cold, gusty wind. We continued the search with no success and decided to discontinue searching at 11:00 p.m. and continue again at first light the next morning.

As we left the area we made several marks across the dirt roads that would indicate the passage of any vehicles during our absence. We even marked the wire loop that secured a cattle gate to let us know if it had been moved prior to our return. We then went to town and secured the evidence at the fish and game office.

I arrived back at the scene at 7:00 a.m. the next morning. I first checked the road and gate markings to see if there had been any vehicular activity during our absence. All were undisturbed indicating there had been no activity during that time period. I began the search beginning at the road where I took the suspect into custody and followed a trail into the bushes in the general area he exited.

At 7:45 a.m., approximately thirty yards west of this location I found the field dressed carcass of a small yearling male deer concealed under some brush. This was consistent with the suspect being able to carry the carcass over his shoulders while hiking over uneven and rocky terrain. The carcass was cold due to ambient temperature well below freezing but was in a fresh condition. Some body fluids, still in a liquid state were pooled in a protected part of the body cavity. I noted what appeared to be a bullet hole on the right rib cage area that looked to me like an entrance wound. I could find no corresponding exit wound. I was grateful that there was no evidence of any kind of predator disturbance noted.

I didn't move the carcass so the other warden who was to meet me in a short time could also see it in its' present condition. He met me at 8:30 a.m. and filled me in on his activities after he left me the night before. He picked up our arrestee from the police department and transported him to the sheriff's jail where he was booked and held to await bail to be set by the judge. While at the jail he had the deputies remove the rest of his blood stained clothing, bagged it and maintained it for evidence purposes.

I then took him to the carcass so he could also see the size and condition prior to moving it. We then secured the carcass in the camper shell of his pick-up, then back tracked the subjects travel from the evening before and followed them to a rocky area just beyond where I first spotted them. We found dried blood splattered on some rocks and on the dirt and soon located the partially buried entrails from the field dressing procedure. The interior organs were checked for a bullet but none was found. The liver and heart were bagged and retained as evidence. Observations of the entrails also confirmed that they were from a small male deer. We returned to our pick-ups and the deer evidence was tagged and retained by my partner warden.

Later that day the carcass and bagged organs were placed in a secure evidence locker freezer where they were held pending the disposition of the case and use in court if necessary. Before leaving the scene he turned over to me the additional clothing evidence from the suspect, jeans, plaid shirt and a t-shirt. We both left the scene but spent the rest of the day writing the reports and diagramming the activities that would show distances and relationships of my observations and evidence collection sites. Remember the golden eagle? I also had to feed her and make sure she was doing okay. My family also helped with this fun chore.

The following month, when the suspect, through his attorney, entered a "not guilty" plea at his initial court appearance I began the additional investigative steps to prove the guilt of the defendant in a yet to be scheduled court or jury trial.

The evidence that was collected and still secured had to be tested by different agencies depending on their expertise. For example the deer carcass, entrails, saw and clothing were delivered to our own wildlife investigations laboratory for further examination by a pathologist. The initial work was to locate the bullet that was thought to still be in the muscle of the inside left front leg. A .22 long rifle bullet was located and removed. The tests of the carcass, entrails or gut pile, and of the blood on the clothing revealed that they were of the same genetic pattern and all were common to blood from the carcass and gut pile. The hairs from the outer clothing were identified as deer hair from a deer in winter coat.

Next I took the three rifles and the recovered bullet to our state department of justice where a criminalist also identified the bullet as a .22 long rifle and further that two of the submitted rifles had different class characteristics that ruled them out.

The Winchester Model 67 was test fired in the lab. The bullet submitted from the deer matched in both class characteristics and individual markings and in the opinion of the criminalist was fired from the same rifle, the rifle identified as belonging to the suspect.

I maintained possession of all the evidence submitted and secured them again in our evidence storage facilities to await trial.

Let me tell you about the "trial". The legal proceedings went on for fifteen months plus I had a little bonus surprise at the conclusion but I'll get there later. The first was a "motion to suppress" all the evidence by the defense. That motion was denied. Three months later the first two day long jury trial resulted in a hung jury. I later found out some questionable decisions were made by a few jurors. Five months later the next two day long jury trial was held and the result this time was "guilty as charged". The defendant was sentenced to fifteen days in county jail, $350 fine, forfeiture of his rifle and no hunting or accompanying other hunters in the field for two years.

My little surprise was a lawsuit filed against me by the defense for my alleged mistreatment of the defendant while he was in my custody. That went nowhere and was dismissed but it was filed by some in the local court system that I had to work with for the duration of my career and it took awhile for some of that pain to go away.

What began as an investigation into "just some gunshots" in an area where they may be legal took well over a year to be resolved. While this case could be considered "routine" in the life of a game warden it illustrates that observations of witnesses aren't always as we might believe they might be.

CLOSED SEASON TROPHY HUNTERS

This case also occurred during closed season for the take of deer. It was reported by an acquaintance of mine but I want to explain a little more about him and his family and the people who sometimes go out of their way to report an observed violation or at least a suspicious circumstance that could be a wildlife violation.

In this particular case the report came from someone that I had a prior law enforcement contact with. Let me say that we did not become great friends but during our "history" we developed a genuine respect for each other that came from honesty, fairness and a respect for wildlife and their habitats. There are times when wardens are called to investigate cases or situations that while being a violation they are unintentional or accidental. We all know that "stuff" happens but if understanding and leniency can be part of the contact, the warden may gain an ally for the future. This was the case here. In fact being fair and not judgmental and willing to give a break when I feel one may be "allowable" helped me develop several witness-informants during my career.

The actions of two local men that prompted this citizen report and investigation was observed by such an ally and his family. An actual violation was not seen but because the area is deer winter range and at this time of the year is populated by large concentrations of deer, and due to the actions of the two men observed by him and other members of his family, they suspected illegal activity had taken place.

I got home from a night patrol at 4:15 a.m. this Sunday morning in late January. Mid winter had been a good time for me to work nights targeting illegal spotlighting, mainly for furbearing mammals that either were out of season or prohibited to take anytime. I slept some then returned to work at 10:00 a.m.

I contacted some fishermen at a local reservoir then checked an area nearby where I knew a trapper had a short trap-line for beaver.

My supervisor received the initial report of suspicious activity north east of town and relayed the information to me by radio at 2:30 p.m. I was given information concerning the reason for the report that included a vehicle description, license number and direction of travel of the suspicious acting men.

I responded a short time later driving the only road which was a direct route to the area. The suspicious vehicle, a sedan, passed me going the opposite direction. I reversed direction and stopped the vehicle at 3:00 p.m. Two local men were in the vehicle. I told them that I was following up on a report of suspicious activity that may have involved them. I had them get out of the vehicle and we continued our discussion while standing on the dirt road side shoulder. I did not separate them but let them describe to me what they were doing in the area and what actions may have been seen by witnesses as illegal.

Their combined and most likely rehearsed description was; "we were in the area on foot trying to call coyotes from a blind. There were some does in the area but we didn't shoot at any deer. We took a shot at one coyote but apparently missed because we couldn't find it. After searching for the coyote we decided to walk back to our car and while walking back we found an old set of bleached deer antlers."

Both were dressed in full camouflage. They each had a rifle, one in the front seat belonging to the passenger and the other in the trunk. Both were cased. Also on the front seat was a manual animal call common for calling coyotes to an injured rabbit. I made a cursory check of the rifles to ensure they were unloaded and inspected the interior and trunk of the car, and obtained identification including

hunting licenses. Having seen no evidence of a violation or evidence that they had shot a deer I released them and they continued toward town. One bit of evidence that they were not aware that I gathered after they left was photos of their footprints they left in the dirt.

I turned around and once again headed toward the area described by the witnesses. When I got to the gated road that led up the hillside to the area, I was contacted by the witnesses. They were a local family that I knew from prior contacts as I described in the first paragraph of this chapter. They immediately said that the two men I had contacted at the vehicle were the same two they had seen acting suspiciously. They offered to show me the exact location of their observations so I followed them in my pick-up to the area. They first showed me where the suspicious car had been parked. They stayed at my vehicle while I confirmed that the same two men exited then entered their car by comparing the footprints I noted during the earlier car stop and conversation I had with them. The witnesses then directed me further up the hillside where they used a boulder outcropping as a landmark. This was about a quarter of a mile from the road. We all got out and walked to that spot through low brush and rocks. The witnesses said the driver of the car, who was the larger of the two, was seen carrying something to the boulder area. Again I confirmed this information with the footprint evidence left in the dirt. I followed the footprints to the back side of the boulder and saw the head of a male deer partially hidden under some brush and sticks.

I told the witnesses to stay back from this area so I could reconstruct the suspects' activities which appeared at this point to be illegal so it was now a "crime scene". The head was fresh, still warm, and the blood had not coagulated. The head had a fairly heavy 6X4 point antler rack and had been skinned and removed from the carcass using a method called "caping". This method is used when future mounting of the "trophy" head and antlers is the desired goal.

My investigation continued and was fairly easy as I followed the same footprints about two-hundred yards to the large carcass of a headless male deer. It was also warm and very fresh and compatible to the head. Also notable was that the carcass had not been gutted and no attempt at "field dressing" was seen. It was in this area I saw both sets of footprints again and they showed that both men had been involved in the butchering process. Scattered around on the ground was lots of blood stained paper towels. I did not see the knife or saw that they would have used. I took the air temperature and the temperature of the carcass to be able to prove time of death if required later. I took photos of the footprints here as well for comparison purposes. I collected the head for evidence and I returned to my pick-up.

It was now 5:15 p.m. and I contacted my supervisor to advise him of the status of the investigation and that I was en-route back to town. I asked that he contact the two suspects and request they meet us at the fish and game office. I and the witnesses then left the area.

I thanked them and advised them of my findings and returned to town arriving at 6:00 p.m.

I contacted my supervisor who had the driver of the car with him in the office. He was read his rights and pretty much repeated the same story I heard from them a few hours earlier. He agreed to answer my questions saying he knows nothing of a deer violation. I first told him the story the way the evidence clearly illustrated the truth. I was honest and left nothing out.

He then admitted that he and his partner killed the deer to get the trophy head. He said his partner shot the deer with his Ruger.22-.250 rifle with one shot. They removed the head, hid it by a boulder planning to retrieve it later. But they changed their mind after my contact with them along the road from fear of being caught. I asked about the knife and saw and he told me his partner has the knife and they hid the saw in some brush because they couldn't get it clean. He continued to tell me that the rifle used was the one I saw earlier in the front seat area of the car. He then wrote and signed a statement for me describing their deer poaching activity.

My supervisor left to contact the other suspect at his home. He returned with him a short time later with the rifle, knife and the boots he had worn earlier. He was reunited with me in a different room, advised of his rights, and then I repeated the same "factual" story that I told his partner.

He admitted participating in the same poaching activity as previously described by the other suspect. "I shot the deer with my rifle

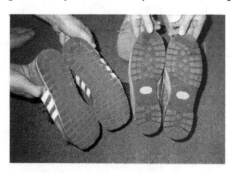

with one shot because my friend wanted it for a trophy." He also wrote and signed a statement describing their poaching activity. I photographed the soles of the boots he brought in that he had been wearing and also the soles of the tennis shoes that the first suspect was wearing. The rifle and knife were held as evidence.

I then brought them together and told them of the results of the investigation and issued a citation to each of them for; taking deer during the closed season and waste of game as they had no intention of saving any of the meat. They were cited to appear in court and released.

At 9:15 a.m. the following morning I returned to the scene with my supervisor. The deer carcass was relocated and checked for additional evidence. Some bullet fragments were collected from the area of the one bullet wound and held as evidence. We removed parts of the carcass to be preserved as evidence and for comparison to the head then I looked for the saw that was supposed to be hidden nearby. I found the hacksaw only twenty yards away. It had lots of blood, hair and dirt on its' blade and the upper strap had prints that may be useful if a trial was demanded. Lots of additional photos were taken of the evidence and the area now that the light was better.

Two weeks later they appeared in court and pled guilty as charged and waived time for sentencing. I did not even have to appear. Each were fined $907, given forty eight hours jail time, 100 hours of community service, three years probation and loss of hunting privileges for one year. The Ruger M77 .22-.250 rifle with scope that was used was forfeited to the state. I was pretty satisfied with the sentence.

One additional response from one of the suspects, the one that shot the deer, occurred three days later. He delivered a Hallmark "Thank You" card to our office addressed to me. He quoted from scripture and thanked me for doing my job. He wrote; "as a christian our contact regarding my illegal activities was God's way of showing me that He will not stand for compromise in a person's walk." Galatians 6: 7-8; "Do not be deceived: God cannot be mocked. A man reaps what he sows. The one who sows to please his sinful nature will reap destruction; the one who sows to please will reap eternal life". This was a pleasant surprise for me. I had the opportunity to contact many fellow christians during my career, many of them on Sunday mornings and some even from my home congregation. Some contacts were informational, friendly encounters but there were some that took me to the next level of wildlife law enforcement.

"WE DIDN'T SHOOT THE DEER, JUST TOOK SOME MEAT"

I went home for lunch on another Sunday in December just before noon. I didn't make it to the food because of a phone call. I received a report from a citizen who I didn't know, about his finding a deer carcass earlier the same morning. He lives outside of town and right in the middle of a portion of deer winter range that is a popular area for deer feeding in their winter habitat. He was attracted to the carcass by ravens and magpies who always signal "a meal of dead meat" by their presence.

I contacted him and he took me to the dead deer. As we approached, several ravens, magpies and a golden eagle flew from where they were feeding. He had no additional information for me. He heard no shots or saw any suspicious activity in the area. When he left, I continued my investigation.

The carcass was fresh and appeared to have died the day or evening prior. Just a side note here about determining how long a deer had been dead. Taking the body temperature of fresh kills can help with this. Although not scientific another thing I would do would be to take a fresh deer carcass to a remote area and return each day until all the evidence was gone. These were carcasses that were not suitable for human consumption and usually obtained from highway kills. I found that five to seven days was all that was required for all sign to be gone. Plus I could see what species of animals were taking advantage of the free meal by tracks and other evidence left at the scene.

Continuing with my observations of the condition of the carcass, the antlers had been removed with a saw and the hind quarters,

shoulder meat and one of the back-straps were also gone obviously removed with a knife. Both sides of the jaw was shattered and appeared to me to be caused by a bullet entry and exit. I took meat and hair samples and photographs of the

carcass and of the general area, including the access roads to the location of the carcass. I found two sets of footprints that went from the dirt road to the carcass and back to the road. I was able to connect them to a distinct vehicle tire track that I thought was made by a full-size pick-up truck. I photographed and measured the footprints and tire track.

I then contacted a seasonal biologist who I knew was conducting a study in this area about deer mortality due to mountain lions. She told me she was in the area yesterday until early afternoon and saw no evidence of scavenger birds indicating a fresh deer carcass. She told me she saw two adult males shooting shotguns at an old abandoned dump site about a quarter mile away from the deer carcass area. She was able to describe the full size pick-up they had and said she remembers seeing a similar vehicle in the area at other times.

I then re-checked the tire tracks and saw that the same vehicle made at least two trips along the road adjacent to the deer carcass. I went to the old dump site where I saw the same tire tracks at the place the biologist had seen the pick-up the day before. So that gave me a pretty good vehicle description plus very good tire tracks to help with my investigation.

I drove to a small residential neighborhood close by to see if I could locate a pick-up that fit the description. Ten minutes max and I had it! It was parked in the driveway of one of the houses.

While walking to the front door of the house I couldn't help but notice deer hair on a red stained area of the truck bed. There was no tailgate, just a net across the rear of the bed. A woman answered the door and I asked to see her husband. She said her husband  was asleep but she would get him. While waiting for him to come to the door I walked back and forth in front of the house and along the dirt driveway. I saw some small pieces of red meat that appeared fresh along with the hair and red stain on the bed of the pick-up. The footprints alongside the pick-up matched those found at the carcass and the tire track also matched those from the road near the deer carcass and from the old dump site.

After a short wait, five or ten minutes, a young man came to the door. I recognized him from prior contacts I had with him and his dad and he recognized me and I'm sure he knew the reason for my "visit". We began with some small talk about the truck ownership and about how long he lived in this particular area and then I asked about his activities the day before and specifically who may have been driving his truck. At this time we slowly moved from the house to the driveway. He said he and his wife are the only ones' who drive it.

He told me he spent a lot of time the day before driving "all over out there" indicating a large area of deer winter range that included the old dump site and the area where the deer carcass was. I asked if he saw anything unusual and he answered "just lots of deer".

I asked if he saw any dead deer during his travels and he answered "no". I asked if he had any deer in the bed of his truck the past few days and he said "no" but continued by telling me the last time he had a deer in the bed of his truck was during deer season about two months ago. As we approached the rear of his pick-up I asked him if there was any reason why there would be fresh deer sign in the back of his pick-up right now and he said "no".

I then told him of my investigation of the deer carcass I conducted over the past three hours leaving nothing out. I picked up some of the deer hair and a small piece of meat from the bed then we walked to my pick-up where I placed the hair and meat into evidence bags. Again I told him that I was following a trail of evidence, that being my reason for being there. He immediately responded, "We did take the meat off that deer, we didn't kill it".

Here's how the first "story" went. "Me and my friend were driving along the road just before dark and saw the deer because six or seven coyotes took off running from it. I walked over to it and saw that the horns were cut off and it was already cut open and its' throat was slit. I cut off some of the meat from the front and hind quarters and put it in the back of my pick-up". He told me that he had all the meat because his friend didn't want any of it. I told him that I would have to take the meat. He led me into his house where he removed six packages of meat from the freezer in the kitchen. His wife was preparing to leave in the pick-up so I asked if I could check the truck completely before she left.

We went back out to the driveway and he opened the doors and a tool box across the front of the bed. I found a small piece of fresh meat in the right side of the toolbox. Across the rear window in a gun rack was a Marlin .22 lever action rifle. I removed it and found it to be unloaded. There were some bullets in the cab for the rifle. I asked if he had the rifle with him yesterday when they found the deer and he answered "yes". I secured the rifle in my pick-up, took photos of the rear, the bed and of the tires and allowed his wife to leave in the truck. I asked him where the antlers were and he again said they were gone when they found the deer. He granted me consent to search his house and the rest of the rear yard area.

He accompanied me to the rear patio area where there was a large ice chest with blood stains on the outside and some wet blood pooled in the inside. He told me they used the ice chest to carry most of the meat. While still in the backyard I again asked him, "where are the antlers?" He answered, "I've got the horns in the house in the kitchen". I followed him back to the kitchen and he removed a 3X3 set of deer antlers from a lower cabinet that was full of pots and pans. The skull portion was wrapped in a dish towel and damp with blood. I asked how I could contact his friend. He gave me his name and said, "All he did was help me cut it up, that was it".

He kept talking, saying that the deer was down and he didn't know if it was sick or injured. "He was sitting on his side looking at us and had his tongue hanging out so I went

over and cut its' throat, no way he was going to make it". I asked if the deer had a little .22 hole in it somewhere and he replied, "No sir". I gathered the rest of the evidence including the ice chest and antlers, gave him a receipt, and also my card asking that he have his friend contact me.

I returned to the deer carcass and spent another hour looking for additional evidence and taking additional photos. I finished up and returned to town to where I photographed, tagged and secured all the evidence. A short time after finishing I received a call from the friend who said he got the message to contact me. I told him I would like to talk to him and he offered to meet me at the fish and game office the afternoon of the next day.

We got together the following afternoon and I told him of my investigation and of the statements made by his friend the day before. He told me the same "story" that I heard before denying any knowledge of the deer being shot. I figured that they didn't have a chance to speak today so I asked him, "If I told you your friend admitted to me today that he shot the deer would you change your story"?

With this he re-told the story describing that they were on the road in the pick-up just before dark when they saw the buck. It was lying down and didn't react when it saw them. They got out of the truck and his friend shot it two or three times in the head with his .22 rifle. "It was still alive so he slit its' throat and removed the antlers and some of the meat. I helped him carry the meat and antlers to his truck and then helped him take it into his house." He finished his statement to me with, "I didn't want anything to do with it. I knew it was wrong as soon as we got done".

I re-contacted the "main player" in this incident the next day. I told him what his friend told me the day before about him shooting the deer with his .22 rifle. He finally admitted shooting it but said he thought something was wrong with it because it didn't get up when it saw them. After shooting the deer it was still alive so he slit its' throat after which they removed the antlers and some of the meat.

This case concluded with a couple of court appearances. While both subjects played a part in this violation of taking a deer during the closed season charges were filed only on the man who owned and drove the pick-up, owned and shot the rifle, and retained all the meat and the antlers.

He pled guilty and was fined one hundred dollars and forfeiture of his rifle but the part of his sentence that hit him the hardest was the conditions of his thirty-six month probationary period. "You are subject to and must obey each of the following conditions; you will not engage in hunting or trapping, and will consent and submit to the immediate search of your person, automobile, garage, residence, yard and any other place under your control upon the request of any peace officer, for the detection of game or game parts and to obey all laws, city state and federal". For a young man living in a "sportsman's paradise" this was almost intolerable.

ADMISSION OF GUILT BUT VERY LITTLE EVIDENCE

On Saturday at 12:30 p.m., I received information from a neighboring warden, about a deer being killed late in the day the previous Wednesday. It was now two months after the close of the deer season. He got the information from an informant who described the older model pick-up and gave him a partial license number. The informant watched from his parked vehicle quite a ways downhill from the obvious "poaching".

He watched the pick-up going back and forth along a road where there's usually plenty of deer to watch. It was close to sundown when the pick-up stopped and a man left the pick-up and walked up hill and out of sight. The witness heard several shots from what he believed was a .22 rifle and a short time later saw the man drag a small deer back to the pick-up where another man and woman waited for him and helped him load it into the bed.

After receiving the information I and the warden who received the report immediately went to the neighborhood where I had seen a similar pick-up in the past. We found the pick-up and even though the license numbers didn't match it was close enough plus it was parked in front of a house that was familiar from prior contacts so it was a good bet. The resident plus several other people were standing nearby.

I engaged them in conversation while the other warden checked around the area. I directed my questions to the resident. He told me that the pick-up belonged to a friend of his who is presently in jail. (I later confirmed that his friend was being held in jail the day of the violation.) He told me that the pick-up had been used for a few days by a friend to move some personal belongings from town to a house in this same neighborhood and he pointed out another man standing with the others. I then went to him and asked, "Did you use your friend's pick-up?" He said, "I used it to move my personal belongings from my girlfriend's house to a storage trailer behind my friend's house last Thursday and Friday". I went back to the homeowner, my original contact, and asked him when his friend used the pick-up. He said, "He had it all day Wednesday and brought it back on Thursday."

Back and forth I go. I returned to the man I will now start calling the "suspect". I asked, "Is it possible you had the pick-up on Wednesday also?" He said," it was possible but I'm not sure of the days." I got to the point and asked who was driving the pick-up late Wednesday afternoon describing the area where the deer was killed adding that we got a report from an eye witness. He said he did not know.

I asked if we could talk in private and he agreed. We went to the storage trailer and looked inside but nothing of significance was found. I gave him the Miranda warning and he agreed to answer my further questioning. After several more questions and telling him more of what the witness saw he admitted shooting a deer. "I wanted a deer to use for food so I borrowed a .22 rifle and drove around but couldn't find one. I then went to some friends and one of them said he would help me find a deer for some 'pot'.

We went to a canyon in the foothills where we saw some deer. I got out and shot from the road then went up on a ridge and shot some more. I had 12 bullets and I used them all. I went to the area where I thought I hit one and found a small deer down but still alive. I slit its throat and partially gutted it and dragged and carried it back down to the road. I saw a vehicle nearby that probably belonged to the witness".

"We left and went back to my friends' house and finished cleaning and skinning it." I asked where the meat was and he replied, "That's the worst part of the whole thing, nobody got any meat. We left it on a table outside overnight and the dogs got to it and ate it. We found some remains the next morning but the meat was gone." I asked him what he used to clean the deer with and he showed me his pocket knife. I retained it as evidence as it had some hair that appeared to be deer hair on it. I asked to see the back of the pick-up and he said he steam cleaned it since the deer was in it. I collected some hair from the rear edge of the floor at the tail gate. Then he agreed to show where the hide and head were dumped but there were no remains or additional evidence found.

Two days later I went to the location of the poaching. I found a drag mark in the snow that ended at the road shoulder. I found a spent .22 casing on the road shoulder then continued to follow the drag over a ridge to a flat area. I found the remains left from a field dressed deer, took photos and collected some of the evidence. Nearby I found 11 additional spent .22 casings that made his story complete regarding the 12 rounds he fired.

After completing the report I contacted the district attorney who issued a complaint charging the suspect with taking a deer during the closed season.

CHAPTER 15

OPEN SEASON DEER VIOLATIONS

Game wardens are called upon to work "out of district" during season openers or special hunts in areas where additional enforcement was helpful or needed. This also applied to seasonal fishing openers. For example; a warden whose district did not have deer populations enough to attract hunters could be sent to a district with a large influx of hunters during the deer season, especially during the opening weekend or first few days of the season.

Deer hunting violations during the open season usually were tag violations, the taking of an illegal deer, usually a spike buck, or waste of game referring to the flesh normally eaten by humans. Regulations require that the proper license and deer tag be possessed by the hunter while hunting and upon killing a deer the tag must be immediately filled out and punched with the date and time of kill and attached to the animal. In addition the tag was required to be countersigned by a warden or other peace officer before transporting such deer except for the purpose of taking it to the nearest person authorized to countersign on the route being followed from where the deer was taken. You can't take it home first. Another part of this regulation prohibited possession of a tag or license issued to another person while hunting.

To be legal during the general season in the part of the state I worked, the deer had to be a forked horn or better unless during a special hunt where different rules may have applied. And with any game mammal, the portion of the flesh usually eaten by humans shall not be allowed to go to waste as can be the case when a "hunter" is only looking for a trophy to hang on his or her wall. The head or antlers will be retained and the rest left to go to waste. Therefore it is a violation. I have always considered the heart and liver of deer and elk to be normally eaten by humans. This regulation; however, did not consider the heart and liver as being "normally" consumed by humans so were not required to be retained.

AN ACQUAINTANCE GOING HOME AFTER "UNSUCCESSFUL" HUNT

I'll start this chapter with a tag violation. While it may seem minor compared to actually killing a deer during the closed season, I'm sure you'll see why proper use of deer tags are so important for the game warden and the legal hunter. It was a Sunday morning during deer season. Not opening or closing weekend so activity was pretty light and I was patrolling a dirt road maintained by the forest service about fifteen miles west of town that was a popular hunting area for locals. My first contact was with the occupants of a sport utility vehicle that was coming toward me as if intending to leave the area.

I recognized the driver as a member of the same church I attend but obviously neither of us showed up on this Sunday morning. We stopped side by side and engaged in the usual small talk about other hunters in the area, deer seen, shots heard, etc. He told me they were "heading home, we didn't see any bucks". He was with his son-in-law and he again said they hadn't seen any deer or other hunters in the area. It was a cold, brisk morning and I noticed that his long sleeve flannel shirt sleeves were both rolled up past his elbows while I had a long sleeve uniform shirt and coat on.

As we talked he had his left arm on his open window sill. I saw what appeared to be dried blood on the underside of his forearm so decided to continue with my normal license, tag and rifle inspections. We all exited our vehicles and I found that both of them had valid hunting licenses and tags with them and the rifles in the back seat were not loaded. Still having a problem with the dried blood and his statement about not seeing any deer or other hunters I asked him about what I saw on his arm. He looked at his arm then stated, "I helped an older guy load a deer into his truck while we were at the end of the road".

I said, "Okay, let me just look in the back area of your vehicle and you guys can go on your way". He opened the rear door and I moved a blanket that was covering a dead buck deer, a nice three pointer that was not tagged. How nice. A fellow church member probably thinking the "game warden" was in church and figured he could kill a deer and take it home for someone else to tag. I found out afterward that his wife also had a license and an unused deer tag. Get the picture? I seized the deer and their tags as evidence. What about poaching on Sunday? I guess that's why wardens work every Sunday.

There was no trial or mandatory court appearance. The case was adjudicated by a simple forfeiture of the amount called for on the standard court schedule of fines. They lost the use of their tags for the rest of the season and of course the venison went to people of our community who could use the meat.

DEER DECOY PROGRAM

The Deer Decoy Program became popular with many wildlife agencies beginning in the late1980's. We set up and used an artificial deer decoy to catch violators involved in several different violations as they drove on little used roads, night or day, hoping to come upon an animal that may or may not be in season or legal to take. The violations could be; shoot from a vehicle, shoot from or across a road, use a light to shoot after dark, trespassing and as we found in some cases hunting when intoxicated and driving under the influence. The decoy deer may be a legal buck but as our local court advised us, "Don't use a trophy buck to add enticement to the violators." As time went on the decoys were automated so their head and tails would move adding a more life-like appearance.

The decoy area was no easy set-up for the team. Along with choosing a location that was known for hunter traffic as well as a suitable location for the decoy, we and our vehicles had to be out of view. One vehicle was a "chase" vehicle and was always occupied and ready and had to be tucked in somewhere and hidden in case a suspect vehicle fled after the driver realized he had been caught in a violation. The officers at the decoy location were on foot. One officer was hidden with a video camera and always at the ready to record the activity and normally there were two others at the ready to jump out and make contact as soon as a violation occurred.

We used this tactic during the open archery deer seasons as well and cited hunters for shooting from the bed of pick-ups, and from the middle of roadways. One of the last decoy set-ups I worked resulted in four citations during an archery hunt. One thing that really stood out was the open containers and beers in the hands of vehicle occupants adding to the dangers to enforcement officers who have to make a sudden and loud verbal approach when coming out of hiding to make the contact after a violation was observed. The common violation was arrows fired from the back of a pick-up or from the road. The hunters showed great surprise when their arrow stuck in the side if the decoy without it moving.

ACCIDENTAL AND OTHER INTENTIONAL VIOLATIONS

A spike buck, one without a fork on at least one side of his antlers, was never legal in areas I worked. There were lots of reasons and excuses given when a hunter was contacted with a spike. Some hunters would actually turn themselves in when they knew that they were 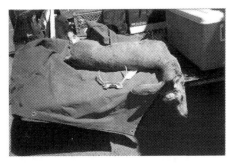 in violation. Reasons could be that it walked in front of the legal buck they were aiming at when they pulled the trigger, or because some of the antlers during the early part of the season still had velvet hanging from the top of the antler and it appeared like a fork on the antler. The velvet could also be cut by the hunter to give the appearance of a branch at the top.

Some of these hunters had witnesses and felt compelled to make the report but others were completely alone with no witnesses but still

"turned themselves in". Here was the opportunity for me to use discretion when making an enforcement decision.

Some would alter the top of the antler by carving a notch with a knife or saw. Alterations were pretty easy to identify as an intentional effort to circumvent the law and would be rewarded with a citation and forfeiture of the deer and their tag for the current season and sometimes for the next year's season.

CHAPTER 16

POACHING MORE THAN ONE MAMMAL

CLOSED SEASON ELK AND ILLEGAL DEER – FATHER AND SON

Another Sunday morning violation(s), this time committed by a father and son from out of town. It was mid way of our deer season and elk season had not opened yet. There had been a bull elk killed two days before in an alfalfa field just off of our main highway south of town. This prompted me to begin my work day concentrating on elk and not deer although they both occur in this same area. The elk killed two days prior had been killed only for its head and antlers and due to the size of the carcass it must have been an impressive trophy. No witnesses or evidence at the scene linked this poached elk to any suspects so far.

I decided to begin this day well before sun rise in an unmarked pick-up and dressed like a hunter. Because this particular elk herd was close to the highway and highly visible I drove to the general area where I would be able to hear gun shots that may come from the area either from deer hunters or maybe from "elk poachers".

It didn't take long for me to hear two rifle shots just at first light. There was no traffic on the highway so I slowly drove onto the roadway and proceeded to the area from where the shots came. I saw a pick-up parked on the road shoulder and as I slowed to pull off onto the southbound shoulder in order to check further I saw two men walking toward the pick-up from the middle of the alfalfa field adjacent to the highway. Right where the elk herd had been two days prior. They each had a rifle and behind them in the field I saw two apparently dead bull elk.

We met at the barbed wire fence near the roadway. The father advised me that they each had shot a buck deer while they were out in the field watching for deer right around sun-up and gestured toward the elk. I identified myself and said I wanted to talk to them back at their truck. So after making sure their rifles were not loaded we walked to their pick-up.

I requested they place their unloaded rifles in the pick-up. In so doing I also saw a 12 volt hand held spotlight on the floorboard. I asked to see their hunting licenses and tags. They had them in possession and handed them to me. Neither of their tags had been filled out or punched as required when killing a deer then I asked if they would accompany me to the downed animals. We climbed back over the fence and they led me to the animals that were bull elk. One was a 3X3 and the other was a 4X3. When I told them that they were elk and not deer and that the season for elk was not open, the father said, "We are new at hunting and we thought the animals we killed were deer." Observing that they didn't appear new to hunting by their clothing, equipment and the normal indication of wear from use of their rifles, I did not believe their "story".

We returned to their pick-up that had a cab high camper shell attached. As we walked to the rear of the pick-up I noticed what appeared to be some dried blood on the outside of the tailgate and on top of the bumper. I asked where they were staying and they said they didn't set up a camp but slept in their truck overnight. They said that they drove from their home about 200 miles away the day before.

I saw two sleeping bags spread out on the bed of the truck that appeared to be full of something. I asked about them and was told "just more of our clothes and equipment". I asked to see the contents of the ice chest that was also in the rear bed of the pick-up. The contents were all normal stuff except for two large packages containing what appeared to be the size of deer livers. Knowing at this point I was being given a real ration of bull, I quit with the niceties and gentle questions and pulled both sleeping bags down toward the tailgate.

This exposed the heads of two does, one carcass in each sleeping bag. Each doe was still fresh enough to indicate to me they were killed not long ago and probably during darkness earlier that morning. "Don't know what a deer looks like, huh?" Further investigation 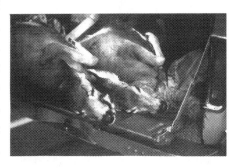 produced a spent casing from one of the rifles on the driver's side windshield resting on the windshield wiper indicating at least one of the elk was shot from the road over the hood of the pick-up. Real winnrs here.

I radioed for assistance from a neighboring warden to help me with the soon to be officially arrested men and help collect the evidence which was no easy chore. I was soon approached by a passing highway patrol officer who asked if I needed some assistance. A friend of mine, he was nice enough to transport the duo twenty miles to the county jail for booking. Being a Sunday, I had to contact the judge at his home for the purpose of setting bail. He set bail at $500 each.

They bailed out the next day and were given an appearance date to answer to the charges. Eight days later they appeared and each entered guilty pleas to the charges of: taking an elk during closed season and taking an illegal deer, a doe during a buck only season. Each was given credit for one day served in jail and was required to pay $750 in fines and penalties. He opted to return the rifles to them which seemed a little strange to me given the obvious deliberate violations that could be called nothing other than "poaching". Here is an example of the benefit of setting a court date so the arresting officer can testify as to the facts of the case. The meat was processed and distributed to the needy of our community.

TAKE OVER-LIMIT ELK – LEAVE ONE TO WASTE, FAIL TO TAG EITHER

Here again, I can't stress enough the importance of observant citizens and hunters who report illegal hunting activity to the attention of fish and game law enforcement.

It was early November and late Saturday afternoon of the opening weekend of elk season when I was contacted by a group of witnesses.

Their report to me was, "we saw an adult male kill a spike bull elk, walk up to it, look at it for a short time then simply walk away leaving it where it lay." They offered to take me to the location so I accompanied them by vehicle to the general location. They led me on foot to the dead elk. There was no one else in the area except the witnesses and it was now dark.

This elk had two spike antlers eight and nine inches long and had an apparent gunshot wound above its' left shoulder. There was no tag attached and no evidence of cleaning or field dressing. It lay at the edge of a field in an area of long grass and weeds so footprints were not readily visible enough for me to identify. This elk was legal to kill, tag and retain in possession but obviously since almost two hours had passed since it was shot I could assume the shooter was not going to return to take care of it. With witness assistance we placed it in the bed of my pick-up. The scenario playing out here led me to believe that the hunter (poacher) wanted a much larger elk that he could brag about and subsequently have mounted by a taxidermist.

The witnesses were able to give me additional information about the shooter. They said that he was the youngest of the group, possibly a teenager. His hunting companions were all older men and he also provided descriptions of two vehicles, a pick-up and a sport utility vehicle that were used by them. And guess what? They even gave me both vehicle license numbers. How cool is that?

I contacted the local police department and asked them issue a "be on the lookout" for the vehicles for me. One showed an address in a neighboring town and the other was not listed so was probably an incorrect number. In any case I checked the local address but could not locate either vehicle. With no additional information received I returned home at 11:30 p.m. and began my night's sleep thinking about my next step.

Back out at 5:30 a.m. the next day, I decided to return to the same general area. First, I knew there were some large elk bulls there and second, I considered returning to the "scene of the crime" and it paid off.

I drove to an area about a quarter mile east of the dead spike elk location. From there I saw parked along a field one of the vehicles described by the witnesses the evening before. It was the sport utility vehicle. I then drove to the location and I saw a small group of men that appeared to be hunters further into the field congregated around something on the ground.

I left my pick-up and contacted the five men. A couple of them were in the act of field dressing a nice 6X6 point bull elk. I saw no tag on the antlers so I asked, "Which one of you is the lucky hunter that has a tag for this nice elk". The small talk to break the ice revealed that only one of this five had an elk tag. He was nineteen, the youngest, and he said he was the one who shot the elk. He removed the tag  from his pocket and proudly handed it to me along with his hunting license. The tag had not been punched and completed with the day, time and method of kill. I kept the tag and license as I explained the tagging regulations to the hunter and the group in general. His rifle, a 7mm with scope was nearby leaning against a bush.

As I was inclined to do I jumped right in to the previous afternoon. I advised them of the witness information and the status of my current investigation. I didn't leave anything out. Their response was pretty fast with three of them saying they were present when the spike elk was shot. The tag holder said, "I shot it but because it was dark when we found it I was unable to get it." I asked him why he didn't pick it up this morning but he had no answer. The oldest of the group who I thought was his father said, "We used bad judgment involving this situation." I thanked him for his honesty and explained that I had picked up the spike elk last evening.

I then told the young hunter that I was going to issue him a citation with three violations; take an over limit of elk, failure to immediately tag an elk after killing it and leave a game mammal to go to waste. This would require my seizure of both of the elk, his elk tag and the only rifle with the group that he admitted using to kill both elk. We completed the paperwork that required a court appearance in about three weeks and included a receipt for the evidence seized. They willingly assisted me with loading the elk into the bed of my pick-up.

A subsequent guilty plea in court resulted in a fine of $1,515 and forfeiture of the rifle he used.

SHOOT SAGE GROUSE CLOSED SEASON AND HUNT DEER IN WRONG ZONE

This was an investigation initiated by a call to our "secret witness program". This program accepted reports from witnesses or informants whose identity was kept confidential. A monetary reward could be issued depending on the outcome and seriousness of the violation. Most callers declined a reward feeling that a "poacher" getting caught and brought to justice was enough. Here is a case where such a person reported that acquaintances of his were planning a trip to hunt in a specific area of our state saying to him upon leaving, "We will bring home something". According to his report they had taken illegal game in the same area on prior hunting trips and said upon returning, "We never see any rangers".

The reporting person, also a hunter and obviously a sportsman even gave his phone number for use by the responding warden if more information was needed. The report was received on the Thursday prior to the Saturday opening of the deer season for the area where they liked to hunt. I was assigned the investigation even though the area was about 100 miles from my residence. I began my investigation by calling the informant and found him to be very helpful with possible vehicle and suspect descriptions and the areas they preferred to "hunt" or "poach".

Due to the distance from my residence I planned to campout fairly close to the suspected area where the violations may occur beginning Friday afternoon with plans to be present before sunrise Saturday morning and Sunday morning if necessary. In order to be able to watch this area for the suspects and remain somewhat inconspicuous, I felt it best to use our "undercover" plain looking pick-up and equip myself to look like just another deer hunter scouting for deer and even doing a little road hunting. I packed my gear and some food and headed out. I can't really call these situations as "camping" because I try to find a location where I can observe the targeted area and the roads in and out while having a place to sleep and the ability to cook a simple meal. However, most times just a cold meal worked in order to be able to respond immediately to suspicious activity.

I arrived in the area late Friday afternoon and watched for similar vehicles that had been described by the informant until well after dark. I then found a place where I could watch and listen and see lights from vehicles if any were in the area. I ate my favorite quick dinner; Spam, cheese, crackers and a granola bar, then settled in to await the morning.

Saturday at 4:45 a.m., I dressed like a hunter, not tough to do after all I hunted deer myself when my schedule allowed, and drove the roads as if I was "road hunting". I continued until mid day and seeing no suspicious vehicles or activity I left to check some surrounding areas where there might be hunting camps. Deer hunting activity in this area was light mainly because the hunting zone was limited and only a restricted number of tags were available from a pre-season drawing. I met with other wardens working areas away from my targeted area to see if any of my suspect vehicles were seen by them. They had more activity in their areas of patrol but no significant violations were observed.

Late afternoon, I returned to my area and checked the roads until dark. I resumed my observations from the same location I used the previous night. Same plan, same dinner and the same quiet night. September weather was usually pretty good before October could bring early snow. I lucked out with very mild conditions.

I began my Sunday morning patrol of the area at 5:15 a.m. as a deer hunter would, looking for deer moving from feeding and watering areas. My granola bar and orange juice breakfast satisfied my hunger as I slowly drove the dirt roads and other off-road trails where vehicles have developed access routes to less traveled locations. I used my binoculars and spotting scope as I slowly traveled looking for signs of hunting or poaching activity.

At 7:15 a.m. while driving up to a vantage point that dropped into a spring fed basin I saw a parked sport utility vehicle that resembled one of the vehicles described by the informant. I immediately saw two men on a hillside close-by, one of them walking toward the vehicle and the other walking further up a hillside away from the vehicle. Both were carrying shotguns. I was stationary as I kept them in view with my binoculars. The man walking up the hillside soon disappeared from my view and almost immediately I heard four gunshots from his location sounding like from a shotgun. I moved further up the road and was able to see him again. He kept walking in a stalking mode and I saw him shoot at a small group of sage grouse. He shot three more times but I didn't see any drop from being hit. He then started walking back down toward the parked vehicle.

The limited season for sage grouse, two days only, had been over for three weeks. I also saw no deer in this area during my two day stakeout.

I continued along the unimproved road toward the spring. After a few minutes I saw the same vehicle with driver and one passenger approaching me on the same road. The vehicle pulled off the road to my right to let me pass and stopped as I got closer. When I got about twenty-five feet away I stopped and exited my vehicle. By now they could see that I was just another "hunter".

I walked to the passenger side door and we made small talk, the kind of questions and answers hunters use when being friendly. The driver, the man I saw stalking and observed shooting at the sage grouse did most of the talking for them. "See anything?" I asked. He said they were hunting deer but didn't see any down in the spring area. He asked me if I had seen any deer and I said, "No, not in this area. Where else have you guys been hunting?" I asked. This was their favorite place was the answer.

While we "chatted" I observed a lever action rifle along the right leg of the driver and a pump shotgun held by the passenger. Enough, I thought, so I identified myself as a game warden and told them what I wanted them to do relative to handling and placement of their firearms. I had them exit the vehicle and told them I wanted to check their licenses, tags, firearms and any game they may have.
They both were very cooperative but given the number of firearms and knives they had with them I definitely was not thinking "routine" so I removed them one at a time from the vehicle.

First the passenger was directed to exit slowly with both hands open and away from his body. There was a loaded .38 Smith and Wesson revolver inside the passenger side door. After a pat down, I had him move to the front of the vehicle. Then I had the driver exit. There was a loaded .357 Smith and Wesson revolver along the inside of the driver side door. After a pat down of him I moved them away from their vehicle for more official investigative questions.

The driver handed me his current hunting license and a deer tag that was valid for a different zone than our present location. Therefore, he was not legal to hunt deer at our present location. The passenger told me, "I'm not hunting deer because I recently had my wallet stolen and in it were my hunting license and deer tag." I asked if they had any game and the passenger said, "I got a bird. There were no deer by the spring but some birds left when we approached so we decided to shoot some." I found one dead sage grouse in the rear of the vehicle in a plastic bag and still warm which the passenger claimed was his. They both told me that they had no idea what kind of bird it was, adding that they didn't know they were not legal to shoot.

I wasn't buying their misunderstanding of the current laws regarding the proper use of deer tags as they have hunted this same area in the past and have been successful. Having a tag for a different area didn't stop them from hunting in their favorite spot during this trip. I then had them stand back further from their vehicle where I could see them while checking the other contents of the vehicle. I found no other game or evidence of additional take of any wildlife during my search.

Both the 30-30 rifle that was beside the driver's right leg and the 12 gauge shotgun that the passenger was holding were loaded

meaning a live round in the chamber, a violation. Also lying across the back seat was another 12 gauge shotgun and a 30.06 rifle both of which were fully loaded. In the far back was an unloaded .22 rifle along with several knives and a machete. I photographed and seized the sage grouse and also seized the 12 gauge shotgun that was used to take the grouse. I also relieved the driver of his deer tag as evidence. I photographed all the weapons where I placed them on the hood of their vehicle. Quite a picture and I issued each a citation to appear in court and gave them receipts for the evidence seized.

We parted ways about two and a half hours after my initial contact I made through my binoculars at 7:15 a.m. Their mandatory court appearance was three months later where they both pled "guilty" to all the charges. The resultant fine was somewhat lower than I recommended to the district attorney. $540 fine and no deer tags to be issued to them the following deer season. Again that last is usually the most severe for hunters or "poachers" to deal with. It may not stop them from illegal hunting but they will look over their shoulder realizing they may be watched. During my contacts with them I never mentioned having received a citizen report of their intended activities. It would have been interesting to hear how their discussion of their trip with their "sportsman" friend went. I guess I could have called him to find out but things got pretty busy for me.

CHAPTER 17

NIGHT PATROLS

These patrols are conducted mostly during fall to mid-winter months and can be planned patrols or just intuitive and decided at the last minute by individual wardens or a group of two or more. I found these patrols to be very active and on target to make worthwhile contacts of poachers resulting in several citations. The local deputy sheriffs also knew our laws so we got "pulled" out of bed many times to complete the enforcement action.

A group of "hunter's" who were really into night hunting formed a club and conducted their own scheduled hunts into various areas of the state. They even had a pre-hunt meeting where certain species of wildlife were listed and became targeted prey for the weekend hunt. These animals were given a point value to be totaled up at their post hunt meeting and illegal species brought higher points. My quote and maybe theirs; "You can't win a contest by obeying the regulations". Showing proof of kill by presenting a part of the animal was necessary to be awarded the points.

The members of this group used pick-ups with modified camper shells, to allow them to spotlight, identify and shoot animals from an opening in the roof where they also carried their rifles or shotguns. Of course our targets were wildlife violations and the middle of the night seemed to be "prime time" for lots of other activities, and not all legal.

Preplanning could mean just getting a good nap prior to being up all night, arranging for a neighboring warden to also be out at the same time mainly for someone to communicate with in a different area. Sometimes we would arrange for use of a department aircraft to be "eyes from above" to direct us to suspicious activity on the ground involving the use of lights from moving and/or stationary vehicles.

With citizens eavesdropping on law enforcement radio conversations by using "radio scanners" I developed a coded location and activity information program that we could use when we wanted to disguise our locations and intentions. For example when this system was used the normal code for "out of service or off duty" or "10-7A" would be reversed to mean "in service and working" or "10-8". We were careful to use this system only with other wardens who knew the codes to ensure our safety. Something else I did especially while working alone at night during a vehicle stop was to indicate that I had at least one other warden with me by using "we" during my conversation and talking back toward my pick-up to an imaginary person such as "I'm okay, you can watch from there", etc.

WOOD CUTTERS AND THE MAGICAL BOXES

This chapter begins with an investigation occurring on a Saturday night late in October, the weekend after the close of the deer season. There were no game mammal seasons open at this time, only upland game where quail was the most popular. A neighboring warden and I planned an all night patrol or "stakeout" where we parked in our patrol vehicles in locations that afforded each of us a view of a very large but different area. We patiently watched with binoculars and spotting scopes for any activity that we deemed suspicious.

Shortly after midnight I saw some flashes of light from a one lane mountain road pretty high on a mountainside across a large valley from me. The road was in a timbered area and was full of switchbacks as it was very steep and recommended for four-wheel drive vehicles only. I could tell they weren't from vehicle headlights suspecting that a spotlight was being used so I maintained watch over the area and advised my partner warden.

He was also familiar with the road but could not see the same suspected spotlight activity so we decided to meet at the bottom of the main canyon where the road began its' uphill climb then join up in one pick-up to continue on. We slowly proceeded uphill with our headlights off in his vehicle. We came upon them a little more than three miles from the bottom of the switchbacks.

We observed two men, each in a separate pick-up, one moving toward us and the other moving away or uphill. They were fifteen or twenty feet apart when they saw us because of our red light to identify us as law enforcement officers and our white spotlight to illuminate them and their pick-ups. They immediately stopped. We split up and each contacted one of the men at their respective pick-ups.

They were local and they recognized us as game wardens. Looking for possible wildlife violations and especially the elements of illegal use of lights while hunting we came up with a 12V spotlight in one pick-up and a 12 gauge shotgun with ammo in the other.

We also saw freshly cut firewood in each pick-up bed and as the four of us talked it became apparent that they were cutting firewood and loading it into their trucks for winter warmth at home or to sell. Not a wildlife violation but my good friends with the forest service would be glad to get the information so they could pursue the federal violation of illegally cutting firewood on national forest lands. While some federal lands are open to "wooding" by permit we were far from such an area and no permits were authorized to be issued.

While I checked the shotgun to see if it was loaded or recently fired I observed some quail feathers on the floor of the cluttered cab. The owner of this pick-up then asked me if he could remove his coveralls as he was hot. I said, "Sure" but closely watched as he did so. I watched as a small wooden box, measuring three and three quarter inches by two and three quarter inches fell to the ground from his right jacket pocket. He immediately picked it up and returned it to his pocket. I acted like I didn't see the dropped box and asked him when he had been hunting last and he said, "I got some quail the day before but there are none in the truck with me now".

I asked for consent to look further in his truck being I saw the feathers and he said I could and offered to help due to the cluttered mess. On the passenger seat in plain view on top of a jacket was another small wooden box measuring three and a half inches by one and a half inches with a hinged lid. I opened it and found a razor blade, small piece of flat glass, some white powder and other white flakey material. He watched as I looked in the box. I advised him of his rights afforded by the Miranda warning, and he said he understood them and that he would answer my questions without an attorney present. I asked, "Who does this box belong to?" His first answer was, "I have not seen it before" thus it must have "magically" appeared. When I refreshed his memory a little by reminding him that it was in plain view on the seat of his pick-up he recanted and told me that it belonged to his buddy who was at the other pick-up talking to the other warden.

He was presently with my partner also having a "question and answer" session. I asked "do you know what is in the box?" "Probably methamphetamines" was his short answer. I then asked him what the small wooden box in his pocket was all about. He said, "My wife gave it to me two days ago and it contains marijuana". He handed it to me and I opened it finding what appeared to be marijuana and also a small white rock with white powder in a clear wrapper. I pointed out the white substance and asked what it was. He answered, "Methamphetamines, but I don't know how it got in the box". Here was another "magic trick" that involved the contents of this second box.

I then went over to the other man and I advised him of his "rights". He also said he would answer my questions. I showed him the box that was on the front passenger seat of his friends' pick-up and repeated what his friend told me. He immediately said, "It's my box and it has illegal stuff in it, methamphetamines".

I asked them when they had last used it or the marijuana and they answered early in the morning the day before. Neither man was visibly impaired. I told both men that a complete report along with the boxes containing the suspected illegal substances would be turned over to the sheriff's narcotics enforcement team for further action. In addition I advised them that their illegal wood cutting activity would be reported to the forest service for action. After unloading the wood they were allowed to leave with us following them to the bottom of the canyon.

The next morning I contacted a member of our sheriff's narcotics enforcement team and turned over the boxes and their contents to him. A presumptive test of the white substance was positive for methamphetamine. He took over the case from this point on. The chief law enforcement officer of the local forest service office was also given the report and he followed up by returning to the area to collect further evidence. I retained possession of my audio tape of the investigation in case it was needed in a court proceeding. The fines and penalties were agreed upon by their attorney's without further testimony or trial.

THREE WEEKS UNTIL FOX SEASON OPENS

This spotlight patrol began at 7:30 p.m. on a Saturday evening late in October. The deer season was open in the area I was working but as hunting pressure was very light I decided to stake-out a remote area where detection of illegal night hunting with use of lights had been productive for me in the past. I was alone and worked the same area the night before but made no contacts. This is how it is with many nights on "lonely" stakeouts. There was no moon and I took up a vantage point and parked where passing vehicles on the two lane state highway could not see me with their headlights. I could see across a valley approximately eight miles and could see several forest service dirt roads that took off from the main road in both directions.

Fifteen minutes after midnight and no traffic observed, I saw a slow moving vehicle that sometimes stopped, then continued toward me continuing down into the valley from the far end. Still at least eight miles away I just watched and kept notes indicating approximate locations where their activity was suspicious. It was below freezing but not too bad considering single digits were probable later into winter. I could see that spotlights were being used with red lenses to shine from both sides of the vehicle to the adjacent fields. They were almost to my end of the valley when they turned off the main road onto a forest service road that led up a steep canyon with a creek running through the bottom. It was now 2:05 a.m. and I was able to continue watching them without changing my location for about a half an hour until I lost sight of them in the canyon.

Without lights, I proceeded to drive up the canyon well behind them but really unsure how far they may have gotten. And like I said it was a clear night with no moon but I had been up this same road many times over the years but rarely without lights. A little out of the "routine" I would say. My plan was to see them before they saw me so I could be very clear about their activities. The road wound through the creek bed in several locations and some ice had formed along the banks.

While concentrating on the canyon walls ahead I failed to notice a large boulder on the left side of the creek. I slammed into it causing enough damage to be noticeable to the bumper and fender but not enough to cause mechanical problems or affect the tire clearance and I thanked God for being with me that whole night.

I kept going up canyon and at 3:45 a.m. I found them shining a white spotlight on the surrounding slopes while they slowly proceeded up canyon. They were using a cassette tape in a 12 volt "varmint call" with outside speakers to attract their prey into the open for a killing shot. I got right up to them and lit them up with my red light. I couldn't hear what they said but could imagine. I recognized the pick-up and knew this was not the first time this truck and owner had been contacted while hunting at night. Maybe the third time and each time the contact resulted in citations. The two men in the truck were both local men and we knew each other from our prior "official" visits.

The three of us met at the rear of their pick-up. Two dead recently killed gray foxes were in the bed of the truck still bleeding. In the cab were three 12 volt handheld spotlights, one with a white lens and two with red lenses. Also a 12 gauge shotgun that had two live rounds in its' magazine, a scoped rifle and a handgun secured in a holster. After explaining my observations and pointing out their violations and my intentions and without asking any questions they told me, "We know the law and are aware that we are in violation". I asked if they knew when gray fox season opened and the driver stated, "In three weeks" and added that "We were just being greedy". They each admitted to killing one of the foxes. I cited each of them for multiple violations, seized the evidence and we both left the canyon returning the way we came with them in the lead. I got home at 6:00 a.m.

After a couple of hours sleep I returned to work, securing the evidence to be held and preserved as necessary for a court proceeding if necessary. First thing the next morning, Monday, I made the appointment to get my patrol vehicle repaired.

After guilty pleas in court, the driver of the pick-up was fined $765 and forfeited his two spotlights and the fox. His violations were; illegal use of a spotlight and take gray fox during the closed season. His partner was fined $565 and forfeited his spotlight, the fox and his 12 gauge shotgun. I don't recall the bill for the repair of my patrol vehicle but felt it was well worth it.

REPEAT OFFENDER, THREE YEARS LATER

Just before midnight on a Saturday night in the middle of January, I and a neighboring warden were conducting another joint patrol for illegal night hunting activity. We set up surveillance from two different locations in a large valley that was bisected by a state highway and was the same area referred to in the previous case where I cited two night hunters for taking fox during the closed season. As a matter of fact one of the violators from that night was here again doing the same stuff but this time he had a different partner with him, I guess he was being trained.

The other warden was parked out of sight at the west end of the valley. He saw light from a powerful white spotlight being shined across a desert area from a vehicle as it was moving slowly along some dirt roads. He advised me of his observations so I started working my way to his location arriving a little less than an hour later.

Together we watched the activity as the pick-up truck, one that was familiar to me as belonging to a local man who had a history of wildlife violations, continued to the state highway and continued moving on the highway with vehicle lights out but still using the spotlight to light up the countryside. The light was being operated sometimes from the driver's side window and then from the passenger side window indicating at least two occupants. We kept watch as they drove in and out of canyons. We were positioned so one of us had them in sight as they moved through the flat but sometimes hilly desert valley.

After about three hours passed we made plans to get into position to make a safe stop of their pick-up. The other warden was able to get in behind them and as he closed in he could hear the calling of an injured cottontail rabbit coming from an electronic animal caller they were using to attract their intended prey; bobcat, coyote or fox. He lit them up with his red light and they stopped. I joined him and we made contact with the driver, passenger and his younger son. They both knew me and were well aware of the laws and regulations concerning night hunting so we didn't need to have that discussion. They had no handguns with them but had three rifles, one shotgun, three spotlights and a dead coyote. The driver had several unused bobcat tags and did have a hunting license with him. The passenger had no hunting license in possession. Their drink of choice that early morning was Peach Schnapps.

This was the third violation for night hunting the owner and driver of this pick-up was cited for; two described here and the third by a warden that lived and patrolled in a different location. The failure he exhibited to change from his "poaching" ways to a legal and "sportsman's" attitude was reflected in the outcome of his court proceedings.

He was ordered to serve fifteen days in the county jail and given several conditions to follow and obey during the ensuing eighteen month probationary period; prohibited from hunting during this period, prohibited from trapping during the probationary period, prohibited from possessing any instruments or firearms used for hunting or trapping, submit to the immediate search of his residence, yard, garage, automobile person or any other place under his control for the detection of firearms or instruments used in hunting and trapping, prohibited from being in the company of any person(s) engaged in hunting or trapping, and during this period obey all laws, city, county, state and federal, and included the forfeiture of his Ruger Model 77 rifle, scope and ammunition, his animal caller and three spotlights. By my request the rifle, caller and spotlights were to be retained by our department for use in our resource academy for education and training.

CHAPTER 18

TROPHY ANTELOPE, NO OPEN SEASON

PRONGHORN ANTELOPE – ILLEGAL SHOOTING

Another call to our state secret witness report line was from someone who overheard a conversation indicating that a local man, who he knew well, shot an antelope in our state and tagged it with an out-of-state tag. The area of the state where this occurred had some antelope that was managed with no hunting allowed due to the small number of antelope in the herd. This small herd was often seen grazing alongside the main highway in this county.

The warden taking the initial call quickly called the neighboring states that had antelope seasons and found one that had issued a permit for an antelope to the man named in the conversation. This certainly added credence to the information received. A call to the warden whose patrol area included the location of the antelope herd named in the initial report was made. He contacted me to follow up as the suspect lived in my town and lived only a few blocks away from me, in fact I knew him from prior contacts.

Later that same day I contacted the most popular "meat and game processing business" in town. I knew the owner pretty well. He was the main game processor for hunters who opted to have their deer and elk butchered professionally. The evidence in this investigation kept piling up. The antelope head, horns and cape with the out-of-state tag in the suspect's name attached was there along with the rest of the meat that had been cut, packaged and frozen. It was quite an impressive set of horns measuring seventeen and a half inches long.

That evening I advised the warden north of me, about sixty miles away, of my findings and he made plans to contact the suspect early the next day. His subsequent contact with him and the answers he received from his inquiry made for a good story but he could not get the evidence that the suspect spent time in the other state or that he even left our state. Our law stated that when bringing any fish or wildlife into our state a hunter was required to make a "declaration of entry" when crossing the border. This usually occurred at an agricultural inspection station. This wasn't done, plus all non-resident hunters that go to that other state to hunt are required to purchase a conservation stamp upon arrival and prior to hunting as this validated the non-resident hunting license.

When asked about his compliance with these requirements and if he had the stamp he said, "No". His out-of-state license was proof as no conservation stamp was attached. He was issued a citation for the "declaration" violation and paid a fine of $268 to take care of that issue. What our suspect didn't realize was a prohibition on the interstate commerce of wildlife taken or possessed in violation of state law.

We contacted an agent with the federal fish and wildlife service and he made phone contact with our suspect and explained to him this apparent violation of the lacey act which if proven in court could bring a maximum of a year in jail and $10,000 fine. Of course this would be in effect if the antelope was taken in the other state and not in ours. He had a dilemma; heavy federal penalties as opposed to probable lesser state penalties if he admitted to killing it here. None the less the antelope head and meat was confiscated and stored in our department evidence freezer pending further investigation.

I also received some additional information from another local hunter who I knew and respected as not just a hunter but a "sportsman". He had talked to the suspect about a month earlier and told him about the "big buck antelope" that was part of the small herd about seventy five miles north. It seemed like the word was out on this trophy animal so the word also got around when it disappeared.

The day after the suspect spoke to the federal wildlife agent he showed up at our fish and game office and requested to speak to me. I was close by so it didn't take long for me to the get to the office. Upon arrival he asked if I had time to see him. As indicated before, I knew him well from our prior contacts.

Of course I had the time, so we went into a private office where he told me he wanted to talk to me about the antelope he shot. I asked him if I could record our conversation and he agreed to allow it. I began by making sure he was present of his own free will, and then advised him of his rights under Miranda. He said he understood his rights and consented to tell me about the antelope and that he did not want an attorney present.

I'll summarize some of the answers to my questions. He told me the date was in mid September at about 5:30 p.m. and he gave me the exact location where the buck antelope had been seen along the highway. He said he was alone and he shot it with a .22 pistol at forty-five to fifty yards away. I have a feeling that he did not want to tell the truth about the firearm used with the chance that the court may request forfeiture. As we were long past the possibility of forensics to determine the method of take I let it be. After many more questions and answers it was clear that he wanted this matter to be closed once and for all. "I done it and I'm sorry I did it" was his closing statement.

Even though this was a fairly short summary of this investigation, about two and a half months passed from the killing shot to his guilty plea during a settlement conference out of court. The resultant sentence: three years probation, forty eight hours in jail, $4,200 fine, forty hours of public service and a prohibition from hunting any animals anywhere for the next three years. He asked a dumb question during the end of his sentencing, "Can I hunt out of this state?" The judge answered, "If Muammar Gaddafi gives you permission you may hunt in Libya".

CHAPTER 19

DOVE HUNTING DANGERS
AND VIOLATIONS

My initial district assignment as a fish and game warden was in a very popular dove hunting area. Nation- wide, dove season always opened on September 1 and because doves are a migratory game bird their regulations regarding their take are regulated by the federal wildlife agency. My first day of work as a game warden was also September 1 so I was immediately thrown into the fray so to speak and had to be shown the ropes concerning the techniques and prime areas for dove hunting success. I also had to learn about the most common violations and where and when they may occur.

I became confident but not so competent that first year. I remained in that assigned location through two more dove seasons and even though I moved to my second district assignment after that, I was sent back to my first assignment to assist with the enforcement of dove season regulations for two more openers. It was probably during my second year that I became aware of some of the dangers associated with dove hunters

EIGHT HUNTERS IN ONE VEHICLE – SIX CITATIONS

One of the most common violations encountered was the "possession of a loaded rifle or shotgun in or on a vehicle" law. I had an out of area warden assisting me early one morning not long after sun rise the second day of the open season and during my second year at this location.

We were patrolling adjacent to a river on a little used dirt road with lots of vegetative cover. We saw an older model Chevrolet carryall on another dirt road traveling very slow in the same direction as we were but about seventy-five yards away. The two roads converged about fifty yards ahead so I put us in a position to intercept them at that point.

From our observations we could see that there were several occupants and that they possessed shotguns and appeared to be "at the ready" at the sight of a flying dove. We met them right at the point of convergence and startled them as they were concentrating on their hunting activity. We knew that in all probability the shotguns they openly possessed were loaded so it was critical for our safety as well as for theirs that they remain as motionless in their positions as possible and with their shotguns pointed in safe directions.

I loudly hailed the driver and the other occupants, "Stop, fish and game wardens. Don't move and keep all firearms pointed in a safe direction!" The driver responded immediately as did the other seven passengers, all were age eighteen to twenty years of age. Some were located inside and some on the roof. We systematically took possession of each shotgun they possessed and after feeling fairly safe, we had them exit or jump down for identification and hunting license checks.

All six shotguns we checked were 12 gauge and loaded meaning that they all had a live round in the chamber. After issuing citations and having a discussion about the safety reasons for the law we released them to hopefully continue their dove hunting in a more safe and traditional manner. It was our opinions that we helped prevent a serious accident or even death and felt good about the contact. We talked to each other about our safety and if there was a safer way to process through that situation. Probably not, was our decision but we agreed it was not a safe situation.

SHOOT AT DOVES FROM THE ROOF OF A
TRAILER AND MOTORHOME

Enforcing the same law with regard to "possession of a loaded rifle or shotgun in or on a vehicle" I came upon another scary scenario later that same dove opener and along the same river but in a more popular area. There were many camps set-up with pick-ups with campers, trailers, motor-homes and tent campers. This area was popular due to the over flight of doves both in the morning and the late afternoon hours. As was my way of making enforcement contacts when possible, I made observations prior to showing myself and making contact. This helps take the "routine" attitude from my work. It's always a great feeling when I made initial contact and upon asking a question be given a false answer and be lied to only to have me be able to dispute their response. Things quickly quieted down at that point.

It was late afternoon and I took a position to watch activities of hunters on the roofs of a motor home and a large travel trailer that were parked end to end close to each other along the bank of this river making it obvious they were together. I saw shotguns in possession of some of the men on the roofs but what put me on alert more was the cans of beer that were being consumed by these "hunter's".

I was to find out by my experiences in the field that intoxicated dove hunters was more common than with other wildlife that was normally pursued by hunters. Most dove success occurs the first few hours of sunlight in the morning and again in the late afternoon and early evening after some have consumed large amounts of beer in this warm climate. I'm sure they felt the need to remain hydrated while seated or standing at the edge of fields. Using the shade of a tree is optimum in the warmth of the valleys. The doves will be shot at as they fly past. There was no hiking involved.

As I continued watching these hunters, luck came my way with the appearance of a flight of doves over their "illegal hunting platforms". There were two hunters on each roof so I wrote down their descriptions and noted when they fired their shotguns which would be proof of my suspicion of their possession of a loaded shotgun on the vehicle. In addition, if they fired they would be in violation of another law prohibiting the "discharge of a firearm from, on or across a road or other way open to the public".

It didn't take long for enough doves to fly over for me to make the observations I needed to see violations. I saw all four in violation and after a ten minute approach by me in my obvious fish and game pick-up I made contact. Because they saw me coming the shotguns were out of sight lying flat on the roofs upon my arrival.

After some initial lies from them when I asked them of their activities I advised them of my observations and requested they unload their shotguns and come down to the roadway where I was. They responded without complaint. When I advised them again of my observations and of the violations I witnessed I also advised them of an additional problem of "hunting while intoxicated". Sure, they had been drinking beer but they exhibited no obvious signs of intoxication.

I cited them only for the "loaded shotgun" violations and warned them of the "discharge from the road" violations but only after I asked to see their doves in possession. They were within the limit of ten per day and twenty in possession.

SHOOTING TOO CLOSE TO HOMES

Another safety related violation was also very common by dove hunters. I normally positioned myself to be able to make enforcement observations the first thing in my work day when the morning hunt began. This violation is "discharge while hunting a firearm within 150 yards of an occupied dwelling". This violation is very often reported by the home owner or occupants who many times would report having their home hit by shotgun pellets. Almost every day of the opening three days of the season regardless of day of the week, this violation would get enforcement attention by wardens. It is so much better to be on the scene and take care of a violation before a victim, a home owner or occupant, has to make the request for one of us or a member of another law enforcement agency.

USE AN "UNPLUGGED" SHOTGUN TO HUNT DOVES

While observing dove hunters along a canal adjacent to an open field early in the morning of one opening day of dove season I heard four successive shots from a hunter who was about two hundred yards away and partially hidden by some trees. I suspected that the shooter of that shotgun was in violation of the law that prohibited the use of a shotgun capable of holding more than three rounds in the magazine and chamber combined. The four rapid successive shots were obviously from the same gun so I proceeded on foot to make contact with him.

A short time later I located him. During my contact with him I found that he had five recently killed doves in his possession and during my "routine" check of his 12 gauge shotgun found that it was capable of holding six total rounds. I recognized this local man and had knowledge of prior law enforcement history but was not sure of the particulars. I issued him a citation for the violation and advised him to install a plug in his shotgun to restrict the number of rounds to only two in the magazine prior to continuing to hunt. I know he was aware of his violation.

I followed up with the court and when I filed the citation I discovered that he had two prior superior court convictions, both for felony controlled substance violations which prevented him from possessing and having under his custody and control a firearm. Two weeks later I signed a warrant for his arrest on this additional violation which would carry a stiffer fine than the initial violation I filed.

DOVE OVERLIMIT AND CLOSED SEASON VIOLATIONS

In addition to the safety issues discussed in the preceding chapter, there are over limit violations that needed our attention along with some problems hunters had with identification of a mourning dove, white wing dove and ground dove. Our season opened with mourning dove only then a period allowed the take of white wings but never allowed the take of the smaller ground doves. The limit was ten per day and twenty in possession so after two days hunting a hunter was allowed to have twenty doves in possession. A large majority of the hunters traveled at least 200 miles to our area for the dove opener and some probably felt that the twenty dove limit was pretty skimpy considering the miles driven for the hunt. Like I said in the prior chapter the migratory bird regulations are adopted by the federal fish and wildlife agency.

To find a ground dove in possession of a hunter signaled an inexperienced hunter and men hunters usually blamed a possession of one of these on his wife or other young hunter in the family to keep from his own embarrassment. Some of the arguments between husbands and wives got pretty heated. The take or over limit violation was worked by setting up in a position early in the morning where the flight of doves was good. Being dressed like another hunter worked well here although we had to do a "little" shooting ourselves to make our disguise complete and effective. We could even shoot a few for our own dinner.

There were plenty of hiding places in motor homes and trailers and some violators felt confident that their "extra" birds would not be detected. That along with letting them know of my observations usually got me the consent needed for access. There were always some removable panels to things such as water pumps, water heaters, etc. that would be checked.

HIDING OVERLIMITS OF DOVES

Late in the morning of another opening day of dove season, I watched as two hunters cleaned their birds. They seemed to be within the limit and when they were finished one of them lowered the spare tire from under the rear of their pick-up bed. He had no flat tire but the inside of the metal wheel had enough space for hiding their birds. Wrapped in some ice the cleaned birds were placed in the open space in the center of the wheel and it was cranked back up in normal position.

They didn't leave but took a break from hunting. Drinking some beers and talking about how smart they were. The "high fives" kind of signaled this to me as they waited for the later afternoon flight. I left to check some other areas and hunting activity. I always carried food and drink with me so I didn't have to exit the "hunting grounds" for chow. I returned about four hours later hoping to find them. Sure enough, the late flight was in progress and hunters in the area were pretty active, including the two smart ones. While keeping my eye on some others, I allowed them to continue until the action was pretty much over. As before, they got together and cleaned their recent take of birds. When finished they put them in an ice chest, picked up their chairs and other equipment in preparation to leave. About that time the "game warden" showed up with his questions about their success and request to see their birds and check shotguns. My prior observations removed the "routine" from the contact. "We got our limits this afternoon so we are pretty happy". "What about this morning?" I asked. "We got a late start so didn't hunt this morning". I started "playing" with them a little. "Another hunter nearby told me that he thought you had a flat tire this morning here in the same place, is that why you didn't hunt this morning?" They looked at each other, I think expecting the other to reply with a believable answer. No quick answer so I laid my cards on the table.

They left that location about forty-five minutes later with no birds. I seized twenty doves from each of them; their ten dove limits from the morning and their additional ten doves each from the afternoon. I cited them to appear in court or they could pay a fine. A fine forfeiture would be allowed if they responded to the citation due date.

HUNT DOVES CLOSED SEASON PLUS ADDITIONAL VIOLATIONS

On a quiet Sunday afternoon in late August while patrolling adjacent to some open fields and only about three to four miles from my home, I saw a pick-up moving slowly away from my position along a dirt road. As was my normal practice I stopped and watched to see what was going on prior to me being observed. As the truck turned sideways to me I saw a young man seated on the roof of the cab with his feet on the hood near the windshield. As I continued to watch, he fired a shotgun as if at a flying bird. The truck then continued to a grove of trees and disappeared from view.

I slowly made my way to the spot where I last saw the pick-up. I found the pick-up that was now unoccupied and no one was seen in the vicinity. I got out of my pick-up and looked inside. I then heard a shotgun blast about a hundred yards or more away. I quickly checked the pick-up and observed the talons of an owl on the center of the dashboard. Then while watching the field in the direction of the shot I saw two young men running away from my location toward some thick brush along a creek.

I pursued on foot and was able to make contact with one of them trying to hide in the vegetation. I then made several verbal demands for the other man to come out of hiding. He finally came into view and after I ordered him to put the shotgun down he came to where we were standing. I advised them of the violations I witnessed and we then walked back to their pick-up, me with the shotgun in hand.

They were age eighteen and twenty-two and I recognized the oldest as having lived for a short time in the house directly behind mine. I'm sure he recognized me but we had no kind of relationship. Once at the vehicles, I radioed for back-up assistance so I could check the pick-up further.

During our "small talk" both said they didn't have hunting licenses and they didn't have their driver's licenses with them. Soon my back-up arrived, one deputy sheriff and one highway patrol officer. Upon checking the interior of the pick-up, I found several small gray feathers on the floorboard and in a small paper sack were two freshly killed mourning doves. I picked up the owl talons and explained that it was a violation to possess fully protected birds or parts thereof. He had a story about the talons and also that the dove were going to be his dinner as he was "living off the land".

I cited the oldest, who was the owner of the pick-up for taking dove during the closed season and for using a shotgun capable of holding more than three rounds. Also he was cited for possession of parts of a fully protected bird, the owl talons. I seized the dove, talons and the 12 gauge Remington shotgun as evidence. The other was cited for taking dove during the closed season.

The deputy sheriff made his time worthwhile with a citation for marijuana possessed by the pick-up owner that was found in the pick-up. I don't know what he had planned for dinner as his doves were gone. I'm sure he had more dope somewhere to satisfy him.

CHAPTER 20

BEARS AND THEIR
RELATIONSHIP WITH HUMANS

The open season for the take of black bears was during the fall and winter months. No "grizzlies" in our state but some of the black bears were pretty big and could appear to be mean. Average males are 190 lbs and they normally range from 126 lbs to 550 lbs. Attacks on humans are infrequent as most would rather run from a human contact. Even though they are officially black bears they could be a variety of colors. All black, all brown or tan with a mix of cinnamon and even some white colors in the chest and neck areas.

Their danger to humans was initiated by the reckless and stupid things or activities of some people who thought it was cool to put out food for them or carelessly leave garbage available for scavenging bears. Some restaurants went so far as throwing their food waste outside where the diners could watch the bears feed while they fed themselves. While they didn't look for human interaction they learned where easy food can come from especially during the summer months when campgrounds and resorts are in high use. When fed by humans or when they find easy food whether from ice chests, in vehicles and tents, bird feeders, bee apiaries or just plain garbage cans or dumpsters they remember where and return for more

BEAR VERSUS CAMPGROUND MANAGER

vA campground manager at one of the forest service campgrounds about eighty miles north of my residence contacted the sheriff's office of that county to advise them that he killed a bear that was in the campground. My supervisor was notified and he requested I respond the following day to investigate. It was late spring and bear season was not open so I was sent to locate the bear, contact the shooter, the witnesses if any and determine the reason for killing the bear.

I arrived at the campground at 10:00 a.m. the next morning and found a small dead bear along one of the interior roads of the campground near some dumpsters. I had a campsite number for the

manager but he was not there. While looking for the manager I was approached by a camper. I asked him if he knew about the dead bear. He said the manager would be back shortly but that he told him a short time ago that the bear was hanging around most of yesterday afternoon. He tried to chase it away but it wouldn't go away so he shot it.

The manager arrived soon thereafter and after introductions he said, "I had to shoot the damn thing you know, I felt bad about it". I asked him to tell me what had occurred that caused him to shoot the bear.

He told me he first saw the bear yesterday afternoon on top of a garbage dumpster when returning to his campsite in his truck. He said he chased it off the dumpster by using his horn. It returned a short time later and he was able to chase it away this time by beating a pot and pan together. Thinking that it might return he armed himself with his 30-30 rifle and sat in a chair at his campsite. About two hours later he again saw the bear in a vacant campsite across the campground road from his site. "The bear stood up and looked at me and started coming my way, kind of nonchalantly wandering towards me you know, so I shot him, the little suckers are persistent, he wasn't afraid of nothing." He said he dropped the bear with one shot as it was walking on all four feet towards him in his campsite. He wasn't sure where he hit it. He told me it was still in the same place where it dropped dead. I asked him where he was when he shot. He pointed at a large tree at the corner of his campsite and said he used it as a rest when he fired. He told me, "I was afraid that the bear was coming towards me and thought it could do me some harm."

I drew up a diagram showing the distance of his location when he watched the bear walk "nonchalantly" in his direction to the dead bear, ninety-three feet. Then from the tree that he used as a rest for the killing shot and the bear where it lay, was fifty-nine feet. The bear was a young male between seventy-five and a hundred pounds and the only blood I saw was where it lay. I found the spent 30-30 bullet casing five feet from the tree he said he used as a rest. There were two bullet wounds in the bear's head, one appeared to be the entrance and the other the exit wound. This was critical in determining the direction the bear was moving when shot.

I took photos of the area and the evidence and collected all the evidence advising the campground manager that I would discuss the facts of the shooting with the district attorney and get a disposition from him. I also reported the incident to the forest service and forwarded the case information to their representative. Upon further investigation of the wounds and by determining which was the entry and exit wounds I was able to determine that the bear was moving from right to left toward the dumpsters and not toward the campground manager when it was shot.

Later in the week and as directed by the district attorney I recontacted the campground manager and issued him a citation for the illegal killing of the bear. He appeared in court, pled guilty with an explanation and was assessed a fine of $300. I was instructed to return his rifle to him.

PROPERTY DAMAGE CAUSED BY LARGE BEAR

A tourist town about thirty miles from my city of residence in the mountains at 8,000 to 9,000 feet elevation had a large bear population. Its' notable draw was skiing that some years extended to the early summer months as snowfall amounts and late season accumulations could be "dramatic". Lots of lakes and small streams provided for great summer and fall fishing. Deer and bear hunting was also a fall activity and the bear population at times seemed to equal the deer in numbers. This area was a popular camping location with forest service campgrounds abundant around the lakes as were many resort accommodations and restaurants.

For many of the residents the bears were a "valuable attraction" and were a draw to tourists who hadn't seen them up close before. However they were a nuisance to some and in some cases caused property damage. A very large bear started visiting the area of a lakeside restaurant that was adjacent to a campground. He would show up late afternoons and hang around feeding on garbage and whatever else he could scrounge from the campsites.

Then on two successive nights he broke into a large refrigerated store room that was attached to the restaurant. He damaged the large heavy door to gain access where mostly soda and beer was stored. Lots of soda and beer cans were squashed and broken. The owner requested a permit to shoot the bear which I took under consideration. Due to some recent reports received of damage he caused at other locations as well as complaints regarding his increased presence in the campground where he also became a threat to human safety, I discussed the issue with my supervisor. We agreed to issue the permit to the property owner.

The permit was issued and on the third successive night the bear returned and continued his attack on the repaired door and broke it open again. It was after midnight but the owner had previously arranged for a hunter friend of his to be on site. He was secreted in a position where he could make a safe and effective shot if the bear returned to cause damage.

He was able to safely discharge his rifle to shoot the bear. After the kill and as required by the terms of the permit I was called at 12:30 a.m. to respond in order to check the scene and remove the dead bear.

My patrol pick-up was a half ton short bed truck and I needed all the space available to carry it but to get it into the bed was another problem. We didn't know it right then but the bear weighed 626 lbs, pretty big for a black bear, but most likely heavy and fat because of his feeding habits.

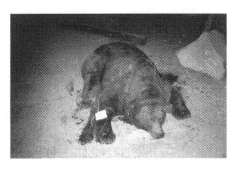

I called for a tow truck and with his hoist and heavy straps around the bear he was able to lift it up and into my truck. I returned home and summoned some help a little later in the morning and unloaded my "cargo" at our fish and game refrigerated storage compound.

TWO BEARS VERSUS TWO WOMEN IN A CABIN

In the same town where the large bear caused problems but now a few years later and mid winter with a few feet of snow on the ground and additional snow in the forecast I got a call to respond to a report from a man who said he was attacked by a small bear. He said in his report that he was attacked while opening the door to his car parked in a designated parking area for the cabins where he was staying. He was okay and said he didn't need medical assistance but was concerned for the safety of others in the area especially children.

I made contact with him later that afternoon and he showed me the back of his right thigh that had a gash about two inches long. It wasn't deep and he again declined medical care. He told me that he didn't see the small bear until it took a swipe at him with a paw. He said there was a female bear, a sow, with her cub in the area and had been seen by many people for several days.

The next day I had a meeting with my supervisor and we understood the need to take action to protect the public safety with regard to these two bears. We were meeting just down the road from the town and it was snowing quite heavily by now. During our meeting we got a call from the local police chief requesting our assistance with an incident involving two bears. From the description of the bears and the location I felt it was the same two bears we were discussing from the incident the day before.

We immediately drove to the area and contacted the chief. The initial report received by the police department was from one of two young women who were staying in a rental cabin. <TNSERT Image31.jpg> The woman said that two bears, a large one and a small one were attempting to break into their cabin at the front door and also at a back window. They were afraid for their safety and felt it wouldn't be wise for them to go outside in an attempt to leave.

We got to the cabin within minutes along with the chief and another member of his department. My supervisor was armed with his 12 gauge shotgun loaded with slugs and I with my rifle. Due to the number of occupied cabins in close proximity we decided the shotgun would be the firearm of choice. He would attempt to get close enough for a shot and I would provide back-up. The bears were still at the cabin and were working on the back window frame trying to get in. Our presence did not bother them.

We got the women out through the front door and into a safe area with the assist of the police. We went to the back of the cabin and were pretty close to them. The larger bear saw us and started running but she was dropped immediately with one shot from the shotgun, thirty to forty feet. The second year bear cub was also dropped with one shot.

We were greatly relieved knowing that these bears would no longer be able to continue their aggressive behavior and be a threat to the public safety. I don't know if the two young women would get a good night's sleep; however, I know I would, knowing that a potentially dangerous situation was over. Thinking back over this situation there had to be a reason for the persistence of these bears. My conclusion is that they had been fed by other recent renters of the same cabin and they returned for more. Dangerous thing to do if that was the case.

CHAPTER 21

MOUNTAIN LION RELATIONSHIPS WITH HUMANS

Many friends and neighbors I had while working as a game warden and even now during my retirement years are curious about mountain lions. They hear stories about them and ask, "Do they live in our community and in our neighborhood, what do they eat, do they only kill for food, and why don't I ever see one?" Let me answer some of these questions then describe some incidents involving this large carnivore that I was involved with.

This large mammal also known as cougar, panther or puma, lives in many different types of habitat nationwide, from sea level to 10,000 ft and in desert to mountainous areas. However; the obvious reason they are most abundant in areas that have a large deer population is because deer are their primary prey. Some studies say that a mature lion requires one deer per week for food. Normally they will make a kill, feed, cover or bury the remains and return for additional feeding later.

The adult male, the largest of the species may be more than eight feet long including their tail and weigh between 130 to 150 pounds. This is in close comparison to the female that can be seven feet long and weigh 65 to 90 pounds. Most people never see this animal in the wild because they are secretive, solitary and very elusive. When getting a quick glimpse of one of these elusive animals the long tail may be the main and only identifying characteristic you'll have a chance to see.

During the late years of my fish and game career the mountain lion designation was changed from "game mammal" to a "specially protected mammal" and as such could only be taken by an agency with public safety responsibilities in order to kill or remove one that was a threat to public health or safety. Also upon request of a property owner who has had livestock or other property damaged or destroyed by a mountain lion we could issue a permit for the take of that specific animal after we investigated to determine the validity of the report.

Before I get into some specifics there was another activity that was very popular during my career, trapping. I have a chapter on this later on but lions became "victims" and many times needed my assistance. When a trapper caught a non-target animal in a steel leg-hold trap or snare he was required to release it. As lions were not legal to take, one that was caught had to be released. I was called upon several times to assist with this fun "chore".

We carried heavy duty "catch-poles" and by properly placing the loop on each end of a lion we could control them enough to release their leg or foot from the trap. Then we would hope they would run off in a direction away from us. Here are some incidents that should give you an idea of the life and habits of this large cat.

DEER HUNTER VERSUS LION

I'll call this a "public safety" incident that I investigated. Deer season was open and it was late morning when I got a call from our office to contact a hunter at his residence. He lived in town and I met him at his home where he told me about an encounter he had early that morning with a mountain lion. He was still dressed in his hunting clothes and boots. He was still somewhat shaken when he told me of his "encounter".

He described to me that while hunting deer about ten miles from town in a remote hilly area on public land he was slowly walking and sneaking around the base of a large rock outcropping where he could get into a position to observe a clearing in hopes of seeing a buck. He sensed movement about ten feet above him on the rocks. When he turned and looked up he saw a lion just above him in a position he perceived as being prepared and ready to spring or jump down onto him. The hunter said he was able to turn and face him with his rifle pointed up at him. "He didn't move but I sensed he was going to jump down at any time so I fired and killed him with one shot."

The hunter told me that he realized it was unlawful to kill a mountain lion but thought he had no choice. I asked if anyone was with him or if there were any witnesses and he said not that he was aware of. I asked him to take me to the scene so we both got into my pick-up and drove to the area, then hiked to the location of the dead lion.

Upon arrival I asked him to stay far enough back so I could look at the tracks and other evidence that may be available for me to compare with his description of the incident. This included such things as location of the lion, the lion and hunter tracks, spent casing and direction the lion was facing when he was shot. My inspection of the area showed evidence that matched with his initial description to me. The fact that he reported it when no witnesses were in the area led me to believe that he was being truthful to me.

He helped me get the lion down the trail and into the bed of my pick-up then I dropped him off at his home. I thanked him for reporting the incident while knowing that it was illegal to kill a lion. I advised him that self protection where immediate danger was perceived by him and attack was very possible his action was called for. In my opinion no enforcement action was warranted and I wished him good luck with his future deer hunting.

LION VERSUS THIRTY-SIX DOMESTIC SHEEP, OR WAS IT LIGHTNING?

This incident provides an answer to the question; "Does a lion kill only what it intends to eat?" Early one summer morning after an overnight rain storm with lots of thunder and lightning I was contacted by the owner of a herd of sheep that were grazing on a hillside just above 7,000 feet and fifteen miles from town. He said the herder reported to him that he found several dead sheep when he checked the herd at first light that morning. He told him that there was a terrific lightning storm overnight and he didn't know if lightning had been the cause of the sheep fatalities or not. I told him that I would respond and contact the shepherd to see if I could determine the cause.

I met the shepherd about an hour later and he led me to several dead sheep that were scattered around the area lying where they were killed. We found ten. He felt responsible for them as any good shepherd would and I told him I would check the area and try to determine the cause of death. The first few I checked had bloody holes in the back of their necks as well as on their throats. I also identified mountain lion tracks at the dead sheep. I called the office and asked for a wildlife biologist to assist me with the cause of death determination of each sheep and to assist with locating additional sheep that may be out of sight in the brushy areas.

Another game warden and two biologists came to assist with this task a short time later. Without describing our investigation step by step I think a summary of our findings and conclusions will suffice.

Thirty-six total dead sheep were found all having the distinct evidence of having been killed by a large mountain lion. During the search and investigation of additional sheep found there was no evidence that any were partially buried or concealed for food at a later time. None of the carcasses had been fed upon and the lion tracks seen at the kill sites were consistently similar in size. The rest of the sheep moved on to a different grazing area later that day and there were no more lion incidents reported in this area.

Before leaving the area we discussed the possible reason for this attack. The only answer we could come up with was that the intensity of the electrical storm caused the lion to respond in this manner maybe thinking that he was under attack.

LION VERSUS EIGHTY FIVE POUND ALASKAN MALAMUTE DOG

An acquaintance of mine called me at home one morning to tell me his dog, a large eighty-five pound Alaskan malamute was attacked by a mountain lion at 12:35 a.m. that same morning. He told me he was awakened by the squealing of his dog that was chained to a dog house fifteen feet from the front door of his home. He went outside to check and saw his dog in the grasp of a "huge" mountain lion. He shouted at the lion from five feet away and it released the dog and ran from the area. The dog received major wounds and gashes in the throat, neck and chest area and the vet told him he may not survive his wounds.

The location was about ten miles from town and at an elevation of 8,300 ft. in an area of some forest service campgrounds and a vacation resort open for recreational use during the summer months. There had been several lion sightings in this area the past few years so the presence of this lion and its' attack of this easy prey could be understandable. While at the scene I was able to identify the area of the struggle and the tracks left by the lion.

We discussed his options in this case and he did not want a permit to kill the lion at this time. Meanwhile his dog appeared to have survived the attack but would remain at the vet's for a few more days of follow-up care.

The next morning at 8:00 a.m., I got another call from the dog owner. He told me that the lion returned to his house the next night probably looking for the dog. There were tracks on the front porch that were preserved in a heavy frost and the dog house was moved from its' blocks and the rug that was inside the dog house had been removed. Knowing now that his dog survived and would be returning home he was concerned about its' future safety.

He reconsidered his prior decision about a permit to kill the lion. I arranged to meet with him later to issue him a permit. The permit was not used as the lion did not return. At least he was not seen again and there were no further attacks reported of any domestic animals in that general area but later that summer reports of additional sightings were made. His dog probably enjoyed staying inside the home with him from then on.

LION VERSUS EIGHTY POUND PET GOAT

Just about a year after the Alaskan malamute attack, another pet was attacked and killed by a lion, this time in another rural area about twenty miles from the town where I live and also about fifteen miles as the crow flies from the dog attack. So given their range and size of their territory it could have been the same lion. This victim was a pet goat that belonged to a thirteen year old girl. Her ten year old brother also had a pet goat that narrowly escaped death during a separate attack just two nights later.

Here is the story of four nights of agony for a family and especially for two young pet owners. Upon awakening one spring morning and prior to school, the young girl found her pet goat dead and mangled, ripped open by a mountain lion just seventy feet from her bedroom window in a fenced area of the yard. I knew the girls stepfather from prior hunting contacts and he contacted me to make a report and to pick my brain on what to do to protect the other pet goat as well as other domestic animals he had on the property.

I issued him a permit to kill the lion and knew he would come up with a plan. He later told me what they did. They decided to leave the carcass out where it lay, as bait for the next night. The second pet goat remained tied up nearby. Nothing happened the night after the first attack. But the next night was different. The lion returned but didn't go to the carcass instead he went to the remaining live goat. The cries of the goat alerted them and their screams and shining lights scared the lion away but not until he was able to claw the goat high on its' side but not seriously. The lion returned again the next night, was shot at and missed but again disappeared into the dark of night. The next morning at the crack of dawn and after lots of phone calls, a couple more of his friends, one who brought a hounds-man with his dogs, entered the picture.

The rest of this story went quickly because of the expert tracking of the lion by the dogs and their handler. It was located a short time later, not too far away and the permit was completed with the killing of the lion. The second pet goat survived the attack and I'm sure the boy's sister got another goat to care for. They will have a mountain lion story to tell their friends for a long time.

LION VERSUS THREE PET SHEEP

I received and responded to a mid-winter morning report from a resident of a rural ranching area not far from town. This area was popular with people who kept farm animals as pets or to use for breeding for sale or to provide food for their families and friends. Horses, cows, sheep and goats were the usual species and they could also raise the feed necessary for their maintenance. Being such a great location for farm animals meant it also provided the needs for some wild animals such as deer as well. This area was right on the edge of "deer winter range" which meant that deer migrated here and stayed during the winter months because of the excellence of the vegetation for food. As you have read previously, where there are deer there are mountain lions. Here comes the reason for the call.

He lost two pregnant ewes and a valuable ram he had for breeding was severely injured and had to be destroyed a short time later. One of the ewes was his young daughter's 4-H project so her project came to a quick end. He knew about lions, their sign and habits so I had no doubt about the culprit. I responded and confirmed his findings

so issued him a permit. He killed the lion, a mature 130 pound male the next night. But as he and his neighbors knew the lions' intrusion into their lives would not end with the killing of just one lion.

INJURED LION VERSUS TWO FISH AND GAME EMPLOYEES

I'll finish this lion chapter with an incident where I could have been the victim. I remember well the end result of this encounter. It started with a permit I issued to the owner of several sheep he kept in a corral in a field within our city limits. He lost a lamb and had another seriously injured by a lion.

We met at the corral where I confirmed his report and determined that the cause of death of one lamb and the injuries sustained by the other was by a mountain lion. The method of kill was obvious and there were lion tracks at the scene. He had several more animals in the corral and there were other small farms close by that contained different kinds of animals. One was a field owned by the local high school for their agricultural program where sheep and pigs were kept.

I issued him a permit for the take of the lion after discussing some safety issues that he should be aware of. He said he planned to be at the corral that night in case the lion returned. Like required by all permit holders he was directed to notify me immediately upon taking the target lion.

Early in the morning three days later he contacted me and told me that the lion returned to the corral in the middle of the night. Using his scoped rifle he shot at it but apparently only wounded it. He didn't know where the lion escaped to and was unable to find it that night.

Being advised of the possibly wounded lion early the next morning, myself and our senior wildlife biologist went to the scene to see if we could locate some sign that would help us find the injured cat. We were able to track it across some wide open fields to a dense brushy area about seventy-five yards from a busy road near the hospital. We saw no sign of blood. We had catch poles, a euthanasia drug in a syringe and of course I was in uniform including armed with my .40 caliber semi-automatic pistol.

We located the lion lying in some tall thick brush. We were able to get close enough to place one catch pole noose around a front leg and shoulder. He seemed to be injured but we didn't know how seriously. By crawling, we inched closer trying to assume a position where we could attain control of him in order to administer the euthanasia drug.

Using a burst of energy we didn't realize he had left in him he got up and fought to get to the opening in the brush which was behind me. I was blocking his exit and on my knees facing him. He continued toward to me and I was forced to my back by his advance. I was able to draw my pistol and fire two shots in quick succession, called "double tap" into his chest and neck area. He ended up on top of me but thankfully quite dead. Neither of us was injured and I only had some blood on my uniform. I've been a fan of .40 caliber hollow point bullets ever since.

The bullet fired by the permit holder obviously did not hit any vital areas. He may or may not have survived. After that morning there were no more reports of dead or injured domestic animals in the area. It's always good to know that the culprit was taken care of.

CHAPTER 22

MARIJUANA GARDEN DETECTION

Knowing by now that a game warden's responsibilities takes him or her to all of the remote areas of their state where employed you'll see that because of this they are often times asked for their knowledge of a specific area. Many times for the same reason wardens are asked to assist with actual investigations by other law enforcement agencies of suspected illegal activities. We are trained the same, armed the same and always willing and available to provide assistance when asked.

In addition to this obvious source of information are the reports received by us and other agencies from sportsmen, primarily hunters who frequent secluded areas in search of game birds or mammals. While doing so they can observe various illegal activities and in the case of this chapter, marijuana gardens.

It stands to reason that areas suitable for wildlife can also be suitable for growing illegal marijuana plants as they would be areas with a natural and available water supply. Game wardens' have a role in the detection and identification of anyone responsible for diverting or working within the high water mark of any waterway including springs, creeks, rivers and lakes. When these gardens are not placed or located in natural water sources there may have to be some type of diversion structure or related ground disturbance that would most likely be illegal without proper permits.

Other than receiving reports from "eye witness" sportsmen I have walked into secluded marijuana gardens while checking for fishermen, hunters or trappers along brushy areas adjacent to rivers and sometimes pretty close to town. When no suspects were present I would contact the appropriate law enforcement agency so they could use their time and resources to further investigate.

One summer I was asked to help with searching for suspected gardens in remote areas by joining officers from other agencies in day long pre-planned flights in a military helicopter, actually a "Blackhawk". Summer months were the time for the national guard to train their pilots. For law enforcement to be able to utilize this resource was a great way to locate reported gardens and to scan areas with known water supplies that would make for good growing locations. We found no suspicious sites during this flight although thick, heavy brush could easily mask this activity.

A deer hunter while hunting in a remote mountainous area early one October, discovered a very large marijuana garden and reported it along with its' precise location to one of our local police agencies and agents of the forest service.

After making observations at the bottom of the canyon that accessed the upper area described by the hunter, a plan was developed.

Seeing lots of evidence of recent horse use it was decided to access the area on foot. A team was assembled comprised of members from several agencies, federal, state and county. I was the only officer from our department as the location was part of my assigned area of patrol. The team consisted of ten members and I was one of four assigned to access the site on foot.

We began our six mile hike at the end of a dirt road at the bottom of the canyon. This was a tactical hike requiring us to be quiet and vigilant as we didn't know if any suspects would be contacted or observed. We arrived at the garden site three hours later and found no one while en-route or upon arrival. After advising the rest of the team by radio they joined us at the garden location via two trips by helicopter. One officer remained at the bottom of the canyon for additional security. The entire area was searched in case any suspects were in the area.

We located their campsite that was somewhat protected from view by vegetative cover. A fire pit, some food, camping gear and leveled sleep areas were part of the camp. Also nearby were some fertilizer bags, some empty and some unused, along with some of the usual tools for gardening. The marijuana plants were in various stages of growth and spread out utilizing the abundant vegetative cover and natural features of the terrain. Obviously a well planned project.

During the search, I found a pretty sophisticated irrigation system that used plastic barrels placed in a nearby spring with plastic

pipe leading to an extensive gravity drip system. The system extended throughout the garden area and appeared to require only limited attention, possibly only weekly. It may seem to be a minor issue compared to the "crop" but the work in the natural spring and the related diversion of the flow was also a violation of state law.

It was decided by the supervising agency to dismantle the camp and dispose of the plants by burning on site. The area was photographed as the plants were identified and counted. 500 marijuana plants from three feet to eight feet tall were gathered into one open area. Some were kept for evidence but most were burned on site.

In addition to the plants that were kept for evidence, the camping gear, tools and other items that may yield forensic evidence was gathered and secured for transport to the state crime laboratory for analysis.

No suspects were apprehended or identified but they surely lost a lot of money from the destruction of their crop although this was most likely just one of their illegal sites given the obvious planning, work and knowledge that went into this business venture.

CHAPTER 23

TRAPLINE DETECTION AND SURVEILLANCE

Trapping of furbearing and non-game mammals was a very popular activity at both of my assigned areas right from the beginning of my fish and game career through to the year of my retirement. I got to know many trappers and for various reasons, good and bad. I assisted them when they asked for help and I cited them when they violated trapping laws and regulations.

There weren't many "routine" trapping investigations. Lots of leg work and some investigations covered several days, most of which were unplanned. I'll stress here something that may not be known to anyone who does not trap. When leg hold traps are set by a trapper they are invisible except for the trapper's disturbance of the area. Footprints may be visible, unless they are brushed out, and there could be visible bait. Exceptions are snares set on animal trails or beaver traps set in water at the edge of lakes, ponds or streams.

During an investigation for trapping activity it was critical to know the habitat and habits of the target species. Then following vehicle tracks to a location where footprints would then be followed hopefully leading to trapping activity. The search for traps could be hard or easy depending on the skill of the individual trapper. Identifications of violations can only happen when the trap(s) are located. In some cases I could pretty much tell who the trapper was by his or her methods I learned from prior contacts.

Some trapped as a sport or hobby and some trapped as a commercial venture. I knew a serious trapper who made $30,000 during one trapping season from fall through winter. Some even partnered with their wives. The busiest years I dealt with were the

mid 1970's to the early 1990's. The most common species that were bought by the "fur buyers" were; bobcat, coyote, beaver, gray fox, badger, muskrat, mink, otters, raccoons and pine martens. The most paid for a raw bobcat fur that I was aware of was $426 and the same year a coyote fur brought near $100. Beavers were next on the value list.

I'll start by telling you about the laws and regulations that kept me and other wardens busy during this time of the year. This will help you understand the reasons for having to spend the hours doing surveillance for the detection of violations at just one individual trap site as well as along a trappers' entire trap line that in some cases covered more than one state.

There were three laws that were violated most often and usually tied to the same investigation. Number one was the administrative requirements to possess a trapping license which was good for one year that allowed for the take of fur-bearing and nongame mammals while in season and also for the selling of the raw fur of any such animal. Every trap set or used had to bear a number issued to the individual trapper by the department. It could be stamped into the steel portion of the trap or onto a metal tag attached by wire to the trap. This pertained to all traps, steel leg-hold traps, conibear traps and snares.

Number two required all traps to be visited daily by the person setting the trap and number three prohibited setting a trap within thirty feet of exposed bait in a manner or position to be able to be seen by any soaring bird. For this violation bait usually consisted of feathers, fur, dead animals, most commonly rabbits, or other means of attracting target animals to the trap. Artificial material meant to mimic any of the prohibited bait is also illegal, such as cotton. Scents are the usual attractant that is legal. Traps set at the entry to a "cubby" where the bait is hidden within the rear of a  natural or self-made hole in vegetation or rocks are ok, just so it is out of view of a soaring bird. It was almost always guaranteed that when locating a trap or trap line that was illegal, these three violations would end up being part of the final investigation.

Upon finding a location where I suspected that traps were being used I would look for signs of recent human presence in order to determine if the traps were checked daily. Prior to exiting my pick-up I would change from my heavy boots to light weight moccasins that had no tread. I did this so the returning trapper would not suspect my presence. Sure, he could see my vehicle tracks but not where I may have exited. If traps were located the information about any recent human prints to the sites would be helpful in determining if the traps had been visited daily as required.

Next I would look for signs of "baiting". If I located a trap I would check to see if it was marked with our departments' trap registration number. If it was obvious to me that the trap had been visited as required and no baiting violation was present and the trap was numbered as required I would not bother any other of the traps on the trap line. If the trapper was knowingly violating the law he most likely would not have a registration number or he would not put his issued number on the trap being used in violation. This meant a stakeout to wait for the return of the unknown trapper. Or a timely return on my part to monitor any activity

Going back to the first violation investigated upon arrival at a trapping site, "failure to visit least once daily. I've documented five days without a trapper's visit a few times meaning just a "weekend trapper", not legal. Without a number on the trap(s) it would be very time consuming for me to be able to identify the violator. The obvious reason for this daily check requirement is to release non-target animals in a timely manner and to be able to dispatch a target animal within twenty four hours of being caught. This is the violation that most times requires a multi-day surveillance in order to make contact with the illegal trapper. If, however, the trapper had his trap number on the traps and if it was obvious they had not been visited as required I would collect the trap(s). Then I would contact the trapper to notify him of the violation and probably issue a citation.

Please be advised that since my retirement there have been some major changes in trapping laws that greatly restricted the types of traps that could be used. Many traps were considered "inhumane" because of the pain and suffering they cause. Many were also considered to be "nonspecific" meaning they will capture whatever animal comes to them. Thus leg-hold and conibear traps are now prohibited.

Since rules and regulations can change yearly I include this special note here: do not refer to any of the laws and regulations I have described, quoted or enforced in this book for your trapping or legal use. Refer to the laws and regulations currently in effect in the state where you hunt, fish, trap or otherwise take part in activities that are regulated by that state's statutes.

The laws that I describe in this chapter are the trapping laws that were in effect when I was a game warden and were the most violated requiring lots of patrol time so I will describe some of the violations I investigated.

SPIKE JAWED TRAPS

I remember well the first trapping violation I investigated while stationed at my first game warden location in the early seventy's. It involved violations in two states by two guys occurring on the same day. I was on a "routine" patrol, pick-up and foot, along the bank of a river about twenty five miles from my home, checking for fishermen. The river was the state boundary for my state and a neighboring state. Just checking fishermen? Not really as I got into something new that I needed to learn.

While "just checking fishermen" I also contacted a father and son along the river bank and determined they were checking their trap line. New to the world of trappers, but realizing what they had going on I asked as many questions I could think of without acting too dumb. I hoped they thought I was just a good investigator. They were checking their traps for beaver but had not caught any so far but it was still early in the morning. They had no traps with them so I decided to check their activities from the water as their traps would be set along the bank in hard to find areas. I returned to town and picked up my state issued boat, an unmarked fourteen foot fifty horsepower outboard that would enable me to search more areas along the heavily vegetated river bank.

I returned up river and launched my boat at a ramp pretty close to where I had made contact with them. I began checking the bank mainly looking for beaver sign, usually a bare ground slide where they enter and exit the water. Something caught my eye but on the opposite bank which was the bank in the other state. A yellow and red ribbon tied to some brush along the river bank was obviously out of place and when I approached the bank I saw two steel leg-hold traps set in the water about three feet from the shoreline. I could see a violation right away as the traps had nails welded to the open jaws making them "spiked" jaw traps which were illegal to use in both states.

I continued down river and about six hours after my initial contact I saw them again on our shore line. I watched as they removed a trap from the water then I re-contacted them. This time I planned to be a little more thorough with my investigation. I tied up nearby and contacted them on foot. I saw that the trap they had was identical to the ones I seized from the other river bank. I had some evidence now that they were trapping so I asked to see their trapping licenses. They had none and showed me out of state driver's licenses. I showed them the traps I had in my boat and they admitted that they belonged to them. I told them where I found them and I got no complaint.

They had three illegal traps in their possession so I seized them and cited them for trapping without a license and for using traps that were illegal for taking furbearing mammals. I told them that I would contact the fish and game department from the other state to advise them of the violations. I told them to remove other traps that may be set until they take steps to legalize their activities. I then left the area and returned to the boat launch ramp.

The following Monday I met with a warden from the other state, gave him the traps I seized from his jurisdiction took him by boat to the site of the traps I seized and gave him the information I had including their statement that they had no trapping license for his state either. The address they gave me was a small town along the river close by so the warden was going to attempt contact with them there. He made contact the next day and cited them on my information so I was summoned to appear out of state as the witness for the prosecution. They forfeited their fines in my cases so all went well and as a matter of fact they were fined more in the other state than in my home state. As long as there was justice and my twelve hour Saturday on patrol was productive I was okay with it.

A NEW PATROL AREA WITH MANY MORE TRAPPERS

Two years later but still in the 70's, I was at my next work assignment, which was about two hundred miles away. Trapping was more popular in this new area and became an activity that took up lots of my winter patrol time. This was because we had four-seasons with colder winters that meant that "mother nature" provided furbearers and nongame mammals with heavier and thicker furs much more valuable and in greater demand by fur buyers.

I found throughout my career that when a prize was awarded for the largest fish or biggest buck or elk and prime dollars paid for the raw furs of certain animals the competition factor takes hold and the laws and regulations are seen as "getting in the way". It was certainly so with trapping. I'm not sure why but our group of local trappers were in large part repeat offenders. It was probably because the fine could be covered by the sale of one prime bobcat fur or a couple of coyotes or beavers. You'll see how some of the offenders were additionally "punished" administratively by our department after the court proceedings were completed.

So while one might think that a game warden is out there simply to make contact with sportsmen and to check their licenses and any game or fish taken so they can indicate on their reports that they contacted lots of hunters or fishermen for that days patrol it is not that "routine" or simple. Some days the first contact could prompt an investigation that continued the rest of the day/night and even additional days.

I got to know most of the trappers in my patrol area. The illegal trappers were more visible to me just because their activity in some cases prompted reports from citizens or other trappers. Trapping was conducted close to town as well as in the remote areas of my district but it always was conducted where the target animals occurred in their natural habitat. So by being familiar with the location and habits of the animals they were after helped me. I also had the opportunity to have a co-worker, a fish pathologist that also trapped more as a hobby, give me some great on the job training on the "art" of trapping.

One of these "repeat offenders" came to my attention not long after assuming my new patrol area. I knew him from a contact with him one day while he was in his pick-up parked along a dirt road near his home. He had some questions about trapping so we discussed the trapping regulations including the three most common violations. My next contact with him was three days before Christmas the same year. While patrolling a popular area for wintering deer and in a canyon about five miles from his home I saw a dead flicker hanging from a tree limb three feet above ground. Investigation revealed an unnumbered trap set directly below the dead bird. I located a second trap about twenty yards away that was also unnumbered. I photographed both traps, the illegal bait then seized the traps. On a hunch I went to the area of his home and saw the pick-up parked outside. I made contact with him and showed him the traps and asked if they were his. He identified them as his and asked, "Did someone turn them into you"? I then explained my investigation and the violations. He said he was getting ready to check his traps so I reminded him to ensure that they were legal. I issued him a citation and continued my patrol. I found out a couple of days later that while checking his traps after I left him he shot himself in the leg while trying to kill a skunk that he caught. Trappers are always armed to be able to dispatch the trapped animals although some use clubs. For the citation he appeared in court and forfeited a fine of $130.

I'll summarize the next contacts I had with him and the resultant court and department actions. Along with additional convictions for using unnumbered traps he had two convictions for using exposed bait and three convictions for failing to check as required. His privileges were revoked for a year by the department after three violations then after this revocation period was complete he continued to trap and was convicted twice more of similar violations. He requested a court trial and was found guilty and assessed a fine of $840, one year jail suspended with three years probation. This also resulted in a three year license revocation by the department. I heard the following year that he sold all his traps, at least a hundred of them, to another trapper then he moved to another state.

THREE DAY TRAP STAKEOUT

The traps he sold? Some of them showed up the following trapping season. Another local bought them and used them without putting his own trap number on them. They still had the number from the revoked trapper from the year before so when I found four of them that were set illegally I thought "my friend" from the prior year who was still revoked for two more years was jumping the gun. Would have been "routine" to attempt contact of the owner of the traps because of the number I knew so well. But wanting to know for sure I decided to stake them out. This site was along a canyon with large boulders scattered about. Great bobcat habitat, and a good area for me to sit and wait. Three of the four were illegally baited with rabbit parts and clumps of fur.

I left the area and immediately contacted my neighboring warden who agreed to assist me. He took me back to the vicinity without using the dirt road to the traps. I then hiked cross country to a clump of boulders above one of the traps. I had a portable radio with me and I told my friend I would stay until well after dark then call him to pick me up.

No activity the rest of that day so I called for my ride. While still dark the next morning he dropped me off and I saw that the traps remained undisturbed so I sat in my "perch" and watched and waited. No activity. So now the third violation was solid, failure to check daily as required. My warden friend picked me up, dropped me off at home, then we repeated the drill early the next morning. Finally, mid afternoon, I saw a pick-up coming slowly up the road toward my location. The twenty eight year old trapper got out and started checking the traps.

When I had seen enough I came out from behind the boulders and contacted him. I was in uniform so he knew what was going on. He told me he last checked his traps four days prior and that he didn't take the time to change the trap numbers from the old to his current number. That's when he told me the story about buying the traps from an older trapper the year prior. He did have a valid trapping license and was issued a trap number. I seized the four illegally set traps, issued him a citation and asked if other traps were set in the area. He said "no, I have no other traps set anywhere". I admonished him to clean up his act and to remove any traps that were in violation and he then left. I called for my friend and he came and picked me up. The trapper was fined $400 which he paid without argument; however, our department soon after revoked his trapping privileges for a three year period.

FAIL TO RELEASE A BOBCAT DURING THE CLOSED SEASON

Game wardens in our state didn't always patrol alone. Sometimes it was prudent to team up with a neighboring warden. On this day however; I teamed up with my supervisor. We elected to use an unmarked patrol pickup and plain clothes so we would appear like hunters. We went on a long patrol day about sixty miles from town and on lots of dirt roads. The season for upland game birds was open for quail, chukar and grouse. It was a little early in the winter for trappers to be active as bobcat season had not yet opened. By the way, we brought our shotguns with us just in case we saw some chukar during lunch time.

At 9:00 a.m. we went into an area well off the main road that I knew contained chukar. We followed some pretty fresh vehicle tracks to the end of a dirt road. The vehicle left several tracks, in and out, that appeared to have been made during the past week. Curiosity caused us to check the area where the vehicle had been. The tracks showed that two occupants exited the vehicle and walked fifty yards or so beyond the end of the road. We followed their tracks and guess what? They led us to some trapping activity that was waiting to be investigated.

We found what looked to be a trap set up against the base of a large rock because of the way the ground had been disturbed. But only six feet away and in the open was a large clump of rabbit fur pretty much confirming our suspicion of the presence of a trap. I uncovered the trap and upon checking found no trap number.

We spent the rest of the morning checking further and located four more traps also with no numbers and another with visible rabbit fur for bait. Near one of the traps the ground was visibly disturbed off to one side and a three inch diameter rock had lots of dried blood on it. There was also a clump of fur next to it which indicated to me that there had been an animal recently caught there. Because bobcat season was closed I decided to collect the rock and fur for analysis to determine the species of animal it was from. After collecting five traps and the bait, plus the blood and fur evidence we headed back to the paved road. At the beginning of the dirt road I cleared a six inch wide strip across the road obliterating all the vehicle tracks so we could see later if anyone returned to the trap site.

We left the immediate area but stayed where we could monitor the main road for any traffic. Just as it was beginning to get dark we saw a pickup head up the dirt road toward the location of the traps. It was a Chevy pickup with two male occupants. We followed at a distance with lights off to make sure they were going to the trap site. They went to the end of the road where we pulled in behind them.

We identified ourselves and told them why we were there and what we had found. Upon showing them the traps they said they belonged to them explaining that they trap together and that they each had trapping licenses and trap numbers. They produced their licenses and trap numbers saying that the numbered tags were in the truck but they hadn't put them on the traps yet. I asked about the blood at the area of one of the traps and they said that they had caught two coyotes the past week and they knew that bobcat season was not open yet. They lived about 150 miles away so no telling how many traps they had out between this location and their homes. They were each issued citations for setting unnumbered traps and using illegal sight bait. Each paid fines of $150 and lost their traps to seizure.

Two days later I sent the rock and fur to our wildlife forensics lab where the blood tested positive for the cat family and the fur and hairs were consistent with bobcat. I contacted the district attorney's office and a complaint was issued to each for taking bobcat during the closed season. They each paid another $150 without any question.

Remember the amount paid for a good bobcat fur? $300 plus. Was it worth it to them? Probably but in addition they were denied a trapping license for the following year.

AGAIN, ANOTHER REPEAT OFFENDER

There were many more investigations with violations but I will outline one more. I got to know a local trapper when he called me at home a little after 8:00 p.m. on a snowy December evening. He told me he had a large mountain lion with a front foot caught in a trap in the hills about fifteen miles from town. He gave me a description that indicated the trap and lion were about a quarter mile from a little used dirt road. There was currently no season for the take of mountain lions so he could not legally kill it to remove it from the trap. I contacted our department wildlife biologist knowing that he would be interested in seeing the lion and also my neighboring warden because additional hands would be useful in releasing the lion.

We left for the location at 7:00 a.m. the next morning and arrived about an hour later. The site was obvious due to the disturbance seen on the ground and brush. We found the trap but no lion but its' tracks indicated it escaped the trap and left the area without injury. While checking the location where the trap had been set I saw parts of a rabbit that was illegally used for bait.

That evening I contacted the trapper and told him what we found that morning. I warned him about the use of bait and told him that he did the right thing by reporting the trapped lion to me.

About a year later while checking out a spring area only a few miles from town I found two traps that were set near various rabbit

parts and fur. Their location and condition indicated they were placed intentionally and in violation of the baiting regulation. They were stamped with the number belonging to the trapper that previously called me about the lion. Not knowing if they had been visited daily as required, I put my business card in the jaw of one of the traps, left it, and seized the other. He did contact me the next day so I didn't pursue a fail to visit charge. I told him I would contact the district attorney for a complaint on the bait violation. He contested the complaint and appeared for a court trial four months later where he was found guilty and fined $225 and put on two years probation.

About eleven months later I had occasion to meet up with him again. This time he thought he was being smart by not putting his identifying number on his traps. Not knowing whose they were meant another stakeout. I left the traps late that afternoon and returned early the next morning to see who might return. I used my issued Trail-90 motorcycle that I could hide in the heavy brush along the road then walked a short distance to be able to observe the location. He showed up about five hours later on his own motorcycle and went to the traps. I watched him go directly to the unnumbered trap I was watching. He looked around the area and began re-setting it. I startled him when I approached. He first denied ownership but then realized his actions were pretty obvious. I cited him for one unnumbered trap only. By now he was getting pretty tired of seeing me which was reflected by his attitude and statement that game wardens shouldn't be allowed to interfere with his trapping activity.

No court trial this time, he forfeited his bail of $80 but again that wasn't the end. Our department revoked his trapping privileges for three years that included the next three trapping seasons.

My final contact with him was six years later. At 3:30 a.m. on a Sunday morning while watching for night hunters using spotlights about seventy miles from town in a remote and uninhabited area I observed a vehicle moving slowly along a state road while a bright spotlight was being used to illuminate the fields on each side of the roadway.

The law is clear; it is unlawful to cast the rays of any spotlight on any road, field, woodland or forest where any game or nongame mammals are commonly found while in possession or control of any firearm or weapon with which any of the above mammals could be killed. I made contact with the familiar pickup with two occupants. They had no animals in possession although they were in popular coyote and bobcat country. The driver was familiar to me for past violations and the passenger, the familiar trapper. They each had rifles with them which I seized and I issued each a citation. Both pled guilty and each was fined $975, and put on twelve months probation. Their rifles were returned to them per the court.

CHAPTER 24

REPTILE TRAPPING AND SPOTLIGHTING

To change focus to a different category of wildlife that also have a commercial value as well as a sport and hobby interest we'll talk about the native reptiles that occurred in areas I worked. There were snakes, lizards and turtles and many other members of the class reptile family. Private collectors were pretty common and they traded and sold them among themselves. The collectors that I contacted at their homes designated at least one room of their home to this venture. They would be secure areas and light and temperature regulated depending on the requirements of the species being held. Pet shops were also a source of income for these collectors however; there were rules and regulations for the commercial take, sale, transport, export or import of native reptiles. As with all species of animals there are some that are fully protected, and it was also the case with reptiles.

The most common methods of take for the snakes and lizards found in the area I worked was a large pit that was dug, maybe three feet in diameter and four or five feet deep, where a section of a large plastic pipe was then placed vertically so when a snake or lizard climbed or fell in they could not escape. These pits would be loosely covered with an old weathered sheet of plywood that wouldn't draw attention to passersby but would allow for the reptiles to seek shelter and then fall into the trap.

The other method was attaching lights to the low front bumper of a vehicle that would light up the roadway as the collector slowly moved along warm summer roads. They could then collect whatever was seen. The reptiles would then be placed in pillow cases for transport. Being rattlesnakes was one of their targets wardens had to be very careful when checking the contents of these "bags" or  other containers. Some of the reptiles and snakes had limits on the number that could be in possession. There were some protected species of lizards, snakes, salamanders and a toad that could not be taken or possessed at any time.

CHAPTER 25

CONSTRUCTION ACTIVITIES ADVERSE TO WILDLIFE

Fish and game wardens in some states, ours included, are called upon to monitor certain construction projects or activities under certain conditions. We became involved "when an existing wildlife resource may be substantially adversely affected by such construction or activity". That meant by any governmental agency, state or local, and any public utility. In addition a subsequent section also requires that "any person" also must be in compliance. Realizing that game wardens are not trained as engineers our focus was about any activity that was detrimental to any and all wildlife that may be found in that location.

ILLEGAL CONSTRUCTION AND DIVERSION OF STATE WATERS

When I was first hired as a game warden and assigned to my initial patrol "district", I thought my patrol time would be spent contacting hunters and fishermen. That's what game wardens do, right? But shortly after arrival I inherited, along with my captain a major earth moving project in progress along a large river. A dike was being constructed and an area of the river was being diverted. I thought the dove opener would take up all my time, after all additional wardens were brought in to assist with that.

Large amounts of dirt was being excavated from private property in close proximity to the river and moved to the river filling a large portion of a backwater lake. Our department was not aware of any plans, permits or contact being made to local agencies for approvals. My role was to take lots of photos, and provide written reports reflecting almost daily visits and also to give verbal "cease and desist" orders to the contractor if on the site. My visits to the site were made on foot, across neighboring farms, by boat and by airboat during low water conditions plus some investigation from the air in department aircraft. The land owner and project manager was from a big city and money didn't seem to be an issue with him. I saw the construction superintendent during many of my visits but never the owner until one weekend morning.

I was photographing and documenting some recent work and was walking along a path where there were still some trees standing and we met. I was in uniform and from a prior description I was pretty sure who he was and he obviously knew who I was, the guy causing problems for his project. To confirm, I asked who he was and he took out his wallet and handed me a business card. At the same time falling at my feet was a $100 bill. He looked me straight in the eyes, I picked it up, handed it to him and said "glad to have met you" then left. I never made a big deal of it but it wasn't accidental. The other contacts I had with him were serving him subpoenas and also during subsequent court appearances. I was at that location for three years then moved on to my second assigned area of the state.

This case was handled through the attorney general's office of our state and it took six years to conclude in favor of the state. Our department was awarded $75,000 in damages and the corporation was ordered to restore the area to its natural condition while providing public access.

MOVE A CREEK TO BUILD A SUBDIVISION

Guess what? I inherited another construction project a little over a month after transferring to my new work location. It apparently began a month prior to my arrival and was much smaller that the project I had just left at my last work assignment. This involved the future construction of several homes but required some initial excavation and realignment of a creek that contained a small population of brown trout. Projects like this can pose problems for the environment when regulations are ignored and especially when wildlife and waterways are concerned.

A landowner decided to build a subdivision in an area that was used by hunters, and trappers and a few fishermen. He came up with the idea to build several homes on his property several years prior. Feeling that it was the right time he hired a contractor and between them decided to proceed but without the required plans being submitted to our county. For sure there were no permits issued.

The initial problem they tackled was to realign the creek that flowed through the property so that a cul de sac could be built for access to the proposed home lots. 150 yards of the creek had been relocated fifty feet north evidenced by the total lack of vegetation along the newly excavated stretch of creek in comparison to the portions of the creek above and below the realigned portion of the creek.

My first task was to contact the contractor in charge of the project who was employed by a local construction company. Arrangements were made for him to meet with me the next day. We met at the fish and game office in town and he described to me the project; the work done so far and the work that would continue to the project completion. I advised him of the requirements set forth in the fish and game code that required notification to our department prior to any diversion of or construction involving creek flow, the bed of the creek and or its banks. He said he would relay the information to the project engineer. A short time later the project engineer contacted me and I advised him of the legal requirements. He completed our required "notification" paperwork the same day.

With the filing of the paperwork by another state agency, the water quality board was brought on board and they ordered that repairs to the altered creek bed and banks be completed in order to control downstream siltation discharges. Their personnel continued the observations of the required corrective actions so I could leave it in their hands although I returned to the area many times. At least the contractor knew I was still involved.

A PRETTY BUT UNNATURAL BEAVER DAM

This "lighter" illustration involved the filming of a movie by a major production company. Could have been from Hollywood I guess but that was not of concern to me. They were filming an open and occupied jeep as it was being driven across a thirty foot wide section of a creek and just upstream from a beaver dam.

This was not a natural vehicle crossing area but most troubling to me was there was no beaver dam there prior to their filming. They built it. This area was a popular fishing area for fly and bait fishermen alike and I was amazed that no complaints were heard although it was during the middle of the week and not a weekend with more  activity. Also, this creek had a good population of rainbow trout.

I inspected this new dam making sure I was not in front of an active camera and noted the amount of limbs, branches and small logs that were required for its' construction. I was in uniform so it didn't take long for me to be approached by someone in the crew.

They were breaking for lunch so I had the opportunity to present my concerns, both legally and ethically to them. I was somewhat surprised at their attention to my concerns and their stated cooperation to be compliant. They told me that they were almost wrapped up with the filming in the creek area and that they would remove all of the "dam" construction material by mid afternoon and haul it away. I told them I would return later to check but before leaving I was invited to join them, cast, staff and crew for lunch. I graciously declined.

I checked later that afternoon and could not tell that they had been there. In some situations issuing a citation is not always the best thing to do for the resource. By the way I bought and still have a copy of the movie that was being filmed. A true story and it was all filmed locally.

CHAPTER 26

WATER POLLUTION AND HAZARDOUS SUBSTANCES

From our code that was current the year I retired, here is part of the unlawful acts under this section; "it is unlawful to deposit in, permit to pass into, or place where it can pass into the waters of this state any of the following: petroleum, acid, coal or oil tar, lampblack, aniline, asphalt, bitumen, or residuary product of petroleum, or carbonaceous material or substance..." then to conclude "also any substance or material deleterious to fish, plant life or bird life."

We attended extensive training to assist with the enforcement of this law. Some of the violations were intentional but others were accidental as I will explain. The training subjects were: hazardous materials detection, protection and clean-up including the incorporation of emergency services and first responder awareness. Also instruction was received on how to set up and manage an incident command system for different kinds of pollution incidents. There was a distinction between different incidents such as those that occurred on highways and other government maintained roadways that in most cases were vehicle accidents. These were managed by highway patrol agencies. Incidents that were off road or in areas where pollutants entered or could enter waters of the state would be the responsibility our fish and game agency. If needed, we would assist each other with the investigation and clean-up of any pollutants involved.

While patrolling remote areas or undeveloped areas close to town I made an effort to check vehicles and their occupants. Could be someone in need of assistance; medically, mechanically or could be someone violating any number of laws. Something I found several times was someone draining the oil from a vehicle crankcase, not into a basin or jug but onto the ground.

DRAIN OIL FROM HEAVY EQUIPMENT ALONG A CREEK

One Saturday, while patrolling to a high mountain lake on a dirt road I saw that it was being paved with asphalt. I thought a good idea as rain and snow runoff from the dirt road affected the creek that flowed along the road shoulder. This was a popular fishing area especially for fly fishermen. When I got to a turnout near a large pond I saw the asphalt company equipment parked along the creek. Construction equipment had in the past gotten my attention due to leaking oil or hydraulic fluids. I parked to contact a couple of fishermen. When I

walked to the area between the large asphalt spreader and the creek bank I found two used oil filters on the ground.

It wasn't hard to see where they came from as large, fresh puddles of oil was under the spreader. I photographed the evidence and bagged the filters then shoveled some dirt on the oil to absorb it until it could be properly cleaned up. I contacted the supervisor of the work crew and he quickly responded and took care of the pollutants.

A similar type violation was draining of holding tanks of trailers or motor homes. Seeing one parked "harmlessly" along a road shoulder at noon time didn't always mean just eating lunch. I hope I was able to "train" some of those contacts about pollution. Some just wanted the citation and not a lecture so I was good either way.

CHAPTER 27

ILLEGAL DUMPING AND LITTER

This was our "litter" law: "It is unlawful to deposit, permit to pass into, or place where it can pass into the waters of the state, or to abandon, dispose of, or throw away, within 150 feet of the high-water mark of the waters of the state, any cans, bottles, garbage, motor vehicle or parts thereof, rubbish or the viscera or carcass of any dead mammal, or the carcass of any dead bird." Litter cases can be as simple as tossing an empty soda or beer can away or leaving behind garbage or trash when exiting a fishing or camping spot.

A few litter citations I issued were for tearing, or crumpling up their copy of a citation I just issued and throwing it on the ground in front of me. These situations usually resulted in a physical arrest and ultimate booking on additional charges as things easily got out of control by these irate people. I cited one young man for litter three times over the course of two years. He must have been a real "litter-bug" to be observed three different times by me during the course of my regular duties.

SLOPPY CAMPSITE PLUS A VISIT TO THE JUDGE

Some litter cases were more involved or serious than others. I contacted a sixty one year old man, his wife and young teenage son camped next to a large pond in a brushy area mostly hidden from a nearby dirt road. They had an old motor home that was apparently their permanent residence or "home". The camp was a mess and it was obvious that the trash and garbage was from them. We had a discussion about some common sense issues and the laws concerning litter. Being my first contact with this family I just warned them with the requirement that they would immediately clean up the area and properly dispose of the garbage and trash. They were cooperative during our discussion. So I left but probably being too hopeful.

About two weeks later while patrolling a similar area about a mile away I located another camp by a different pond. This pond was fed by a nearby river and had an outlet that ran by this unimproved campsite. Same vehicle and family and the condition of this campsite was the same as I saw two weeks prior, but worse. Also his attitude was different this time when he saw me. I did a little "snooping" around his camper, located a loaded 12ga shotgun in the cab. Loaded meant a live round in the chamber. I unloaded it, put it in my truck and started our discussion while looking at the mess at various areas of their camp. In addition to the trash and garbage scattered and half buried there was fresh human waste with toilet paper nine feet from the running water of the river. Now I'm looking at a "flagrant" but also "fragrant" violation of this section of the fish and game code. I issued him a citation for litter and included the loaded shotgun violation as well. I photographed the campsite, took an empty bottle of gin that was on top of a trash pile and also seized the shotgun and ammo as evidence. Being they weren't local I thought by seizing the shotgun he would be compelled to appear in court as instructed on his citation. That didn't work.

Six months later a warrant was issued for his arrest for failing to pay a $300 fine. It took just about a month for a warden stationed 200 miles south of me to make contact with him. Through information from other agencies we located the town where he got mail but we had no address. The warden knew his vehicle and physical description and watched for sign of him during his patrols. He saw the motor home parked near a saloon on the main street of this town. He contacted him inside the bar and asked that he accompany him outside where he was advised for the warrant for his arrest. His remark to the warden was, "I remember the incident but I'm not going to pay a fine. I want to see a judge". He was taken into custody and booked into the local jail where eventually he paid his fine and was released. He forfeited his shotgun to the state.

LITTER WITH NAME AND ADDRESS ATTACHED

While patrolling locations pretty close to residential areas but kind of secluded I would look for evidence of illegal take of game. One morning a month prior to deer season I found a couple of bags containing some parts of a doe that had been butchered and dumped. A little scrounging in the bags produced several pieces of mail and other paper items with a name and address for me to follow up with. Lots of reasons from the young man I contacted but not good enough to convince me. Although I couldn't make the case for illegal take of the deer I certainly could make the case for litter. A similar situation led me to find a check book with other household things contained in one of several bags that had been dumped also in an illegal dump site. I called the person belonging to the checkbook and made a deal,

"If you come down here right now and clean up this area I won't issue a citation". I didn't have to wait long and a man and woman showed up. I heard something from the woman to her husband like "I thought you were taking this garbage to the dump all this time".

NATURE CALLED

I still take the heat from fellow retiree's about a citation I issued to a fisherman along a river just below the dam to a popular reservoir. Nature obviously called and he "retired" to some bushes along the river bank. I saw no fishing violations but contacted him to check his license. I asked if he had seen any litter or trash nearby and he said the area looked pretty clean. He said he was having no luck so after showing me his license he started walking back up to his vehicle. I took a quick peek behind the bushes and confirmed my suspicion then met him at his vehicle to issue him a citation for littering. I had a shovel in the back of my pickup so I was able to take care of the situation. I didn't even take a photo.

CHAPTER 28

EVOLUTION OF EQUIPMENT
AND WEAPONS

Examples of technological advances in communication, equipment and weaponry really ramped up during my early and continuing years in law enforcement. But as you'll read at the end of this chapter there have been even greater advances since my retirement. I will also tell you about some of these advancements and changes I noted during my recent "ride-along" with my police officer son.

During my years of "police work" communication changes took place not only with equipment but also with department requirements and innovative violation reporting methods such as "secret witness" programs that provided for cash rewards in some cases. Some of my investigations as a game warden were initiated by this program.

Our home telephone was a land line phone in the early days and had to be a listed in the phone book and available for the public. But we only had to pay for our personal calls. We had no portable radios, pagers or cell phones so we had two methods of communication; a public phone in a phone booth or our patrol car radio that was installed on the center of the floorboard.

No am-fm radios came with our patrol vehicles so each time I would get a replacement vehicle I spent a few bucks and went to Radio Shack and bought and installed my own, antennae and all. Some of us bought and installed a citizen band radio that was also popular with truckers. We used them when working as a team in remote areas where traffic from our department radios could be scanned. We also bought and used portable scanners so that we could monitor other local agencies from home and also have one installed at our own expense in our patrol vehicles.

I got the idea from my military days to install a black out light under the left front bumper of my pick-up for off highway night driving. Another thing we all did when issued a new patrol vehicle was to install kill switches to our interior lights and to our brake lights. Later on when seat belts were in the vehicles we had to figure out how to silence the various alarms related to their use. It seems we had to counter some of the advancements in technology at times.

Mace came on board half way through my time as a city policeman then pepper spray many years later. We didn't know what a ballistic or bullet proof vest was and when the first one's came out Second Chance was the brand I bought for myself. I still have it and it is light weight and contained in a T-shirt. We bought our own flexible lead saps and large heavy flashlights with five "D" batteries. We had no speed loaders for our revolvers just a leather "dump" pouch that carried 6 or 12 rounds to use if we ran out of the six in our revolver.

Our revolvers were carried in unsecure leather holsters, and we didn't think about having available a rifle or shotgun. This of course was the norm for patrol but some activities, such as serving on our police department's first SWAT team required a more practical or tactical uniform and special weapons that we bought ourselves and with that came additional tactical training. Our department was very proactive with this idea that was pretty new at that time, by training and equipping a group of qualified officers to remain ready and available to respond to the additional situations that were very much a part of the mid to late 1960's behavior prompted by social unrest.

When hired by the department I was still in the active reserve with the army that required a commitment of a long weekend each month and a two week assignment away from home during each summer. We were faced with long hours a few days off during this period which prompted my chief of police to write a letter to my army commanding officer asking for my excuse from further reserve obligations. His request was recognized as a real need for our community and was granted. Sometimes I think it would have been more fun hanging out with my army buddies than the dangers we faced on the street during that time.

We outfitted ourselves in army type combat uniforms and provided our own rifles in addition to having to purchase our own handguns; make, model and caliber of our choice, that we also carried while in uniform and out of uniform. Department regulations required that we also carry our handguns off duty while in the city limits where we had to reside. My choice for duty was a Smith and Wesson Mod 28 .357 magnum revolver called a "Highway Patrolman" which I purchased for $63 and carried it into my game warden years until we were issued Smith and Wesson Mod 19 .357 magnum revolvers. Then by my choice I converted to a semi-auto pistol that I purchased myself. My back-up or undercover revolver was a Smith and Wesson Mod 36 short barrel .38 revolver at $52 when purchased in 1966. Both are in very good working order today in fact I still carry my .357 revolver when hunting big game. Our department arranged the purchase of WW2 era .30 caliber M-1 carbines that we could buy for $43 each. They came packed in cosmoline which is a heavy greasy substance used to protect firearms while in extended storage.

A major change occurred in 1989 when I was a game warden. Our fish and game department made a mandatory conversion from revolvers to semi-auto pistols. I was on a firearms committee that researched semi-autos for our use and agreed with many other agencies at that time that a Glock Pistol in .40 caliber would be ideal for us. We were also issued 12 gauge shotguns but still had to purchase our own rifles but within department guidelines.

Right at the end of my police officer years another piece of equipment was required to be carried while on duty and in uniform. It was a small tape recorder (small in those days) to record our conversations and interactions with citizens. One might think that this system was for officer safety reasons but the bottom line was that it was adopted because of many "police brutality" reports filed by the clientele we faced each and every day in our community. The recordings were held in a large VCR type cassette that was carried on the duty belts of patrol officers and after each shift was logged and held in the evidence locker in case a report against any of us was filed or information about a specific contact was needed.

Toward the end of my fish and game years I bought and carried a voice activated mini-cassette tape recorder. It fit nicely in my shirt pocket. Some of the information on investigations contained in this book came from recordings I still have. Of course now departments have the ability to outfit every officer with a very small, lapel type wireless microphone and camera that records all contacts and sends the data to the officer's vehicle whether it is a car, truck or motorcycle. While the recordings are very useful for law enforcement, we all know the news media also finds this kind of information of particular interest.

Now I'll tell you about some of the amazing things I observed and learned recently while with my son on a day of patrol. I took notes as there were so many things I wanted to remember for this chapter. Let's first consider the patrol vehicle which has a computer interface with the department dispatcher. The computer keyboard is positioned within easy reach of the drivers' right hand. A camera is mounted high center of the windshield to photograph a vehicle being checked or stopped. The patrol vehicle had multi-colored emergency lights as well as the ability to shine white spot lights to each side called alley lights, and "take down" lights to the front.

The vehicle identification number is printed on the roof along with a GPS system in place that allows for constant tracking of the vehicle by the dispatcher. The office monitors the location of all police vehicles. Another little trick available is having control of the street signal lights to be able to stop traffic if necessary. The front driver and passenger doors have ballistic plates installed for added protection. The rear seat area is structured for prisoner transportation so the rear windows have steel bars on the inside and a cage between the front and rear seats. The rear seats are plastic for durability and ease of cleaning and sanitizing.

Also installed in the front left area of the windshield and the rear window is the radar unit antennae. I think we all know what radar is, kind of a broad spectrum system that can monitor multiple lanes of traffic in both directions. An additional unit called lidar is hand held and is target specific. It is directed to a specific vehicle to the front and rear and gives a reading of speed and distance. It would take another session with him for me to fully understand the total function. All of the electronics requires the addition of a second 12V battery installed in the trunk. While looking in the trunk I saw a "spike strip" first aid kit, fluorescent vest, traffic cones, fingerprint kit, and other evidence collection items, fire extinguisher and whatever else the officer wants to have while on patrol.

Another innovation I really like is the tactical vest method for carrying equipment that we used to carry on our gun belt that was pretty stressful for the lower back and hips. The primary handgun is still on a gun belt but the vest includes ballistic plates, collapsible baton, handcuffs, taser, extra magazines containing ammo for all firearms, including AR15 and 12 gauge shotgun with lethal rounds as well as "less than lethal" rounds, a body camera and places for carrying additional equipment.

CHAPTER 29

POST RETIREMENT -
WORK OR PLAY?

Should I relax and go fishing and hunting or use my training for security jobs and even environmental inspections required by EPA at several construction sites? I found that there are lots of jobs available if I wanted one.

Just about four and a half years after my retirement, which was early 2003, I decided to join my wife and also seek out a post retirement job. She continued using her expertise in nursing by taking a position with the local hospice not long after we relocated to our new retirement community. When I wore myself out with house work including laundry and indoor cleaning plus my outdoor jobs of cleaning, yard work such as mowing lawns, chopping and splitting firewood plus the fun time spent in my wood shop or on my boat fishing, I decided to see what may be "out there" for me.

I started by searching the want ads in the newspaper and called a number listed under "security officer" wanted. A local man who started his own security agency after he retired from law enforcement answered. We met and he promptly hired me to join his small group of men and women. He contracted for different jobs in our state and in our neighboring state. I worked nights (all night) 6:00 p.m. to 6:00 a.m., at three different locations during my time with him; a residential golf course, a railroad refueling depot that was under construction and controversial by some of the locals and at a major railroad trestle and multi-track interchange. After about a month the "all nights" plus the driving time and distance to all of these locations prompted me to search again for something a little closer to home.

There was a job announcement for animal control officer in the newspaper so I contacted the local agency involved with hiring qualified people to fill various positions in different venues that also included animal control and "security" positions. With resume in hand I contacted the head of the agency to see what might be available for me. The animal control position had been filled but instead, after a short discussion I was issued uniform shirts, pants, hat and equipment with a schedule of where and when I would begin my new security job. I began with another night job but closer to home at a popular resort hotel and marina.

After a couple of weeks working the resort and in large part because of my past law enforcement experience I was moved to a 7:00 a.m. to 5:30 p.m. job, Monday through Friday at the county court house manning one of the entry doors that was set up with an x-ray scanner to screen entrants that were scheduled to appear in one of the several court rooms. This of course included judges, attorneys, witnesses and defendants in civil and criminal cases. It was a good job that gave me a feeling of purpose and accomplishment. After additional training I was assigned to work some days at the health and welfare office to stand by while irate clientele, mainly men, settled financial issues that in most cases consisted of court ordered alimony and child support cases. More long days but still pretty close to home. I loved the jobs until I saw an ad for a security job really close to home, like a mile and a half away. I had to check it out.

I called the number given for the general manager of a private golf course presently under construction and almost within walking distance from my home. He asked to meet with me just off the highway that led to the course. It was a car to car, side by side meeting. Again, with resume in hand and excited about the possibility of employment so close to home we talked for about a half hour. I gave him the copy of my resume and I had my job interview right there. I was willing to take just about any pay he offered because it was so close to home. He asked about me and my law enforcement history and I asked about the requirements of the position. The position advertised was for security officer but at the end of our discussion he asked if I would be willing to help him "build" the security department and accept the position of "director of security". I didn't know at the time but this golf course when completed would be given the title of Golf Digest's best new private course of 2003 as designed by Jim Engh. I would put together the as yet non-existent security department.

I consented to begin the next week after submitting my resignations to my current employers. There was one security officer presently on site who would remain on staff. Our first "guardhouse" was a little portable shack about the size of two "port-a-potties" but with a functional port-a-potty right behind it. The area was fenced and entry was through a chain-link gate.

Within the next two months I hired enough staff to man the entrance gate to the property three shifts per day and seven days a week. This golf course was also the future site of upwards of 300 various types of housing units, a clubhouse, a kids playground, swimming pool and activity center plus a marina at the nearby lake. Most important to us in security was the construction of a fully equipped "guardhouse" which had a covered drive through entry. Because it was a permission only entry into the "gated golf course community" it also had electronically controlled entry and exit gates.

The staff I hired was some good men living in the neighborhood and those I also had met during my prior security jobs, men that would fit well. I also advertised and interviewed men to fill the number of positions needed. Other things I did; purchase uniforms, equipment, portable radios, computer and a vehicle for late night patrols. Of course a policy and procedure manual was needed along with efficient methods to document and track all those who enter the property. The main entry gate was pretty busy during the weekday mornings when more than 400 construction related vehicles would be processed through into their respective construction sites. No time to sit from 6:00 a.m. to 10:00 a.m. on week day mornings. I continued in that position for two and a half years, then I stepped aside because of some changes that occurred due to growth, expansion and with the direction that management was taking.

Two months later I was "recruited" by the construction supervisor for the same owner and offered a different job. This new job involved environmental monitoring of construction site storm water controls and pollutants where erosion and sediment control methods were necessary to comply with county, state and federal environmental laws and regulations especially because this golf course community construction was uphill from a large fresh water lake. You have read in Chapters 25 and 26, Construction and Water Pollution, about the role of fish and game wardens in monitoring and investigating construction and water pollution cases so that this prior training and experience prepared me for this new responsibility. I also took an online college course to bolster my knowledge and attended some local training courses. A pretty good increase in pay and a company pick-up were some of the benefits and as you might imagine outside work in all kinds of weather conditions that was okay with me and the proximity to my home was obviously the final plus.

The job requirements increased for me after a year or so because of the construction start-up of a second golf course adjacent to the first one but twice as big. This new course was designed by Tom Weiskopf and both courses together were advertised as eighteen hole private golf communities. Both courses were definitely "golf cart needed" courses meaning big and spread out over a very large area. I got pretty busy but was able to hire a part-time assistant.

We kept busy with year round monitoring and compliance with our storm water pollution prevention plans and our recommendations for additional erosion control methods to be put in place in areas where our testing results indicated erosion problems. We consistently monitored about fifteen specific sites. Some were to measure the turbidity of the water flowing onto the site but most were to measure the sediments and turbidity of the water flowing from the site. This was done so we could check for the need of erosion control methods as well as for completing the documentation requested by the environmental agencies. We used an instrument called a turbidimeter to measure the readings at each location every day and especially during and right after rain events of one half inch or greater.

The first winter I had to buy snowshoes to enable us to access some of the sampling locations. I had one accident that occurred while trying to obtain a water sample at the location where water flowed onto the construction site at the highest point and just after a pretty good snow storm. I hiked in about a half mile and while attempting to obtain a water sample the snow covered creek bank caved in putting me into the cold, icy water. I was able to get home quickly, change clothes and warm up. I was glad that home was so close by.

When this golf course was completed my job was completed so I went back to retirement. About three years later the course changed hands and a plan for the construction of some homes was developed. I was asked to return and work for the same guy as before who was now the general manager. Same job but part-time which worked good for me, so at seventy one I was back to work once again and am still at it at age seventy three. Only God knows how long I will be able to continue with this opportunity.

As I still work at this "post retirement" job, I continue to be active in a leadership role in our church and even started a security group there as well. For my neighborhood I put together a community firearms safety class and have conducted firearms training if asked for by "young" and "old". I am lucky to have a wife that loves to fish so we get to spend most of our fishing time on our boat we keep in a

slip below our home. I enjoy hunting for deer and elk but I think it is because of the camaraderie with fellow hunters that make it so great. My first post retirement buck from the late 1990's was taken in my new state of residence and while hunting with my brother. I still maintain a strong interest in law enforcement and firearms and take my wife to the woods to shoot to keep us both competent mainly for self defense purposes.

I feel blessed to have been able to write about some of the events that occurred during my life and career in law enforcement and to share with all readers; my relatives including brothers, sisters, children, grandchildren, my friends, neighbors and anyone else who may feel compelled to check this true story out. The past three years have opened my eyes and actually reacquainted me with my memories of events and people related to each and every chapter. I can say this journey was fun and I would have had it no other way. Thank you for reading and if you are a law enforcement officer "please remember the title of this book" and I personally thank you for your service to your community.

Printed in the United States
By Bookmasters